D1047305

Political Profiles
John McCain

Political Profiles
John McCain

Catherine Wells

Greensboro, North Carolina

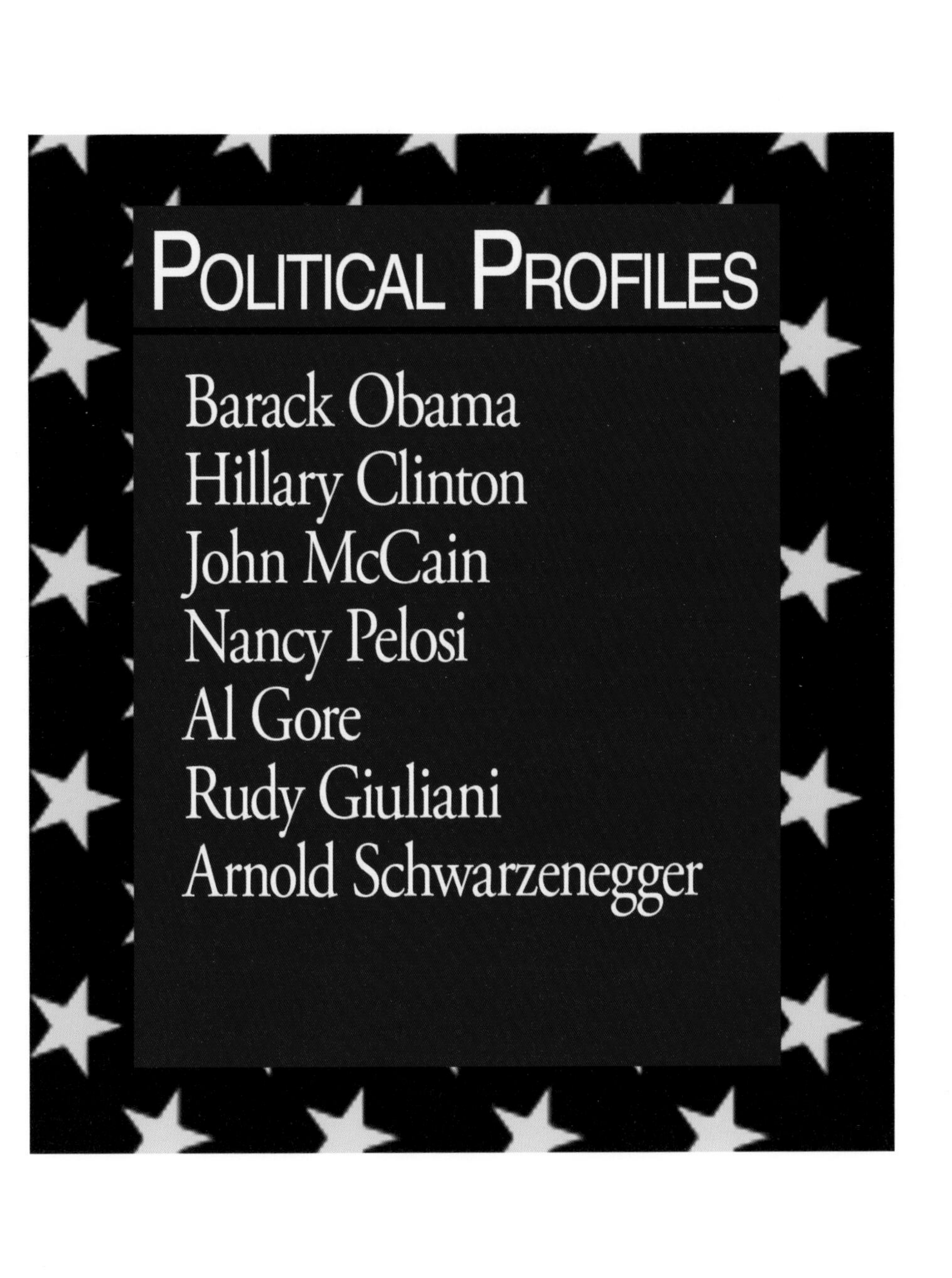
POLITICAL PROFILES
Barack Obama
Hillary Clinton
John McCain
Nancy Pelosi
Al Gore
Rudy Giuliani
Arnold Schwarzenegger

POLITICAL PROFILES: JOHN McCAIN

Morgan Reynolds Publishing, Inc., 620 South Elm Street, Suite 223
Greensboro, North Carolina 27406 USA

Library of Congress Cataloging-in-Publication Data

Wells, Catherine.
Political profiles : John McCain / by Catherine Wells.
p. cm.
Includes bibliographical references and index.
ISBN-13: 978-1-59935-046-2
ISBN-10: 1-59935-046-7
1. McCain, John, 1936- 2. Legislators--United States--Biography. 3. United States. Congress. Senate--Biography. 4. Presidential candidates--United States--Biography. 5. Presidents--United States--Election--2000. 6. Political campaigns--United States. 7. United States--Politics and government--1993-2001. 8. United States--Politics and government--2001- I. Title. II. Title: John McCain.
E840.8.M26W45 2007
973.931092--dc22
[B]

2007027133

Printed in the United States of America

First Edition

Contents

CHAPTER 1:
First Son 9

CHAPTER 2:
Fire! 18

CHAPTER 3:
POW 25

CHAPTER 4:
From Hanoi to Congress 35

CHAPTER 5:
Ascent 46

CHAPTER 6:
Success and Scandal 56

CHAPTER 7:
New World 66

CHAPTER 8:
Maverick 76

CHAPTER 9:
Straight Talk 83

CHAPTER 10:
Another Try 93

Timeline 104
Sources 107
Bibliography 109
Web sites 110
Index 111

one
First Son

When John McCain's grandfather died, President Harry Truman sent his condolences to the family. Vice Admiral John Sidney McCain, known to his family as Slew, had been home from the Pacific theater of World War II only two days when he collapsed, dead from a heart attack, during his welcome home party. Slew McCain had worn himself out relentlessly pursuing and destroying the Japanese navy. One of his fellow officers later said that "He knew his number was up," while he was still in the Pacific, "but he wouldn't lie down and die until he got home."

John Sidney McCain III, called Johnny, was nine years old on September 10, 1945, the day he stood in Arlington National Cemetery and watched the burial of his grandfather. His father, Navy Commander John Sidney McCain II, whom the family called Jack, stood beside his son. After the funeral, the U.S. Congress voted to award Slew McCain his fourth star, posthumously promoting him to full admiral.

John McCain's father, Jack, (right) and his grandfather, Slew. *(Courtesy of the U.S. Naval Historical Center)*

Johnny McCain was born in the Panama Canal Zone on August 29, 1935, where his father was stationed. During the first ten years of his life, until after World War II, when his father had an extended posting in Washington, D.C., his family moved from posting to posting.

The McCains had not always been a naval family. Their roots were on a plantation in Mississippi. McCain's ancestors had owned slaves. It was Slew, Johnny's grandfather, who first left the South to attend the Naval Academy, in 1902. It was a big break from the family's Southern past; Slew was replacing one heritage with a new one.

Jack McCain, Johnny's father, had met Roberta Wright when he was stationed in Long Beach, California. They married in 1935, over her family's strenuous objection, and together began a life of military service—and war.

Jack asked the navy to assign him to submarine duty. When the Japanese bombed Pearl Harbor on December 7, 1941, he was stationed at the submarine headquarters in New Groton, Connecticut.

During the war, Jack commanded a squadron of submarines. He spent part of the war in the Atlantic searching and destroying German naval and supply ships. He also helped support the D-Day invasion in 1944, when the allied armies began rolling the Nazi armies back toward Germany. After the D-Day invasion, Jack and his submarines relocated to the Pacific, where they were patrolling when the Japanese surrendered in August 1945.

Jack was awarded a Silver Star medal, as well as a Bronze Star and other honors, for his war service. But it was Slew McCain, who commanded huge aircraft carriers in the Pacific, who became the most famous McCain during World War II.

When the war ended, and Slew died, Jack McCain was posted to the Naval Department in Washington, D.C. For three years, the family was able to live in one place.

John McCain later said that he could never remember any discussion of his pursuing anything but a naval career. When he was ten his parents, who had long been unhappy with the quality of the education he received in the military base schools, enrolled him in St. Stephens School in Alexandria, Virginia.

McCain stayed at St. Stephens for two years, until 1949. In 1951, McCain was sent to Episcopal High School, an elite boarding school, also in Alexandria. He stayed at Episcopal until he graduated high school in 1954, at age seventeen.

Although it was not a military school, Episcopal helped to prepare McCain for the Naval Academy and the naval career that would follow. First year students at Episcopal were called "rats" and had to serve the upperclassman. They bused the tables after meals, were seated last, and were subjected to mental, and sometimes physical, hazing. The school was all male and most of the students were sons of wealthy and prominent Southern families. McCain was the only military "brat."

Since he was a toddler, McCain had a hair-trigger temper. In the middle of a tantrum he had been known to hold his breath until passing out—usually when he didn't get his way. His parents, driven to distraction by their first-born son's rages, began dousing him with frigid water to try to quell his temper. As he grew older, McCain tried to learn how to rein in his temper, but the problem dogged him into adulthood.

Adjusting to Episcopal was not easy for McCain. He was small for his age, but played football and wrestled. He became one of the best wrestlers in his class, but was never an outstanding athlete. He was better known for the intensity of his playing than for his talent. His classmates remember him priding himself on being a tough guy, always ready for a fight or challenge.

His temper and unwillingness to conform to the rules was a constant drag on his standing, however. There was a demerit system at Episcopal. Punished students had to walk off demerits by circling the quad, sometimes for hours—Johnny McCain did more than his share of quad marches.

McCain rebelled, leaving his regulation tie half-tied and wearing an unauthorized leather jacket when he sneaked into the woods to smoke. When he went off campus, either with or without permission, he would go into jazz clubs in Georgetown and other parts of Washington and try to buy beer, although he was underage. It became a challenge to see how many bars would illegally sell him alcohol.

This adolescent rebellion was only one side of McCain's personality, however. Although he was only an average student, he developed a love of history and literature. He read biographies of famous men, particularly those who had earned their fame on the battlefield or in politics. His favorite teacher, William Ravenel, a former military man who still served in the Army Reserve, taught him to love the works of William Shakespeare, Robert Louis Stevenson, Rudyard Kipling, and other patriotic giants of English literature. McCain liked and respected Ravenel, and Ravenel returned the respect. "I have never forgotten the confidence his praise gave me," McCain wrote years later.

Episcopal High School helped to form McCain's personality and character. He was a maverick, but one committed to age-old values of patriotism, public service, and personal bravery. Many of the other students at Episcopal would enter one of the profitable professions, such as law and medicine; the others would return home to the South to take over the family business. For McCain, his years at Episcopal continued the process of turning him into a naval officer that had begun at his birth.

Although he graduated in the middle of his class—the lower middle—McCain did better than expected on the Naval Academy entrance exams. While the rich naval legacy of his family almost guaranteed that he would be accepted, it was important to him that he do well enough to justify his admission.

After graduating from Episcopal High School, McCain attended the U.S. Naval Academy.

After only a few weeks visiting his family after high school graduation, McCain left for the Naval Academy, located in Annapolis, Maryland. He was seventeen years old.

Though he had done well on the entrance exams, his behavior at Episcopal did not bode well for the much stricter Naval Academy, where there was little tolerance for rebellion. First year students, called plebes, were expected to do what they were told and to speak only when spoken to by a superior. It didn't seem likely that McCain would make it through four years at Annapolis.

In many ways McCain stayed true to form at the Naval Academy. From his plebe year through his final year McCain consistently racked up his quota of demerits. He was also never afraid to speak up when he thought he was being treated unfairly.

In one incident, McCain returned to his room to find the sheets ripped from his bed. Apparently, his company commander thought he had not done a good enough job making it in the morning. McCain did not agree with the judgment and marched into the captain's office. "Captain, please don't do that again. I am too busy to make my bed twice a day." He then turned and walked out. Few plebes were willing to make this kind of risky move.

McCain did excel at one Naval Academy tradition. He always stuck by his word and adhered to the code of honor in his relationships. He never ratted out a fellow plebe or midshipman, and did not complain about the physical training.

Despite his sometimes volatile personality, McCain was a leader—even if he sometimes led his friends into trouble. He led a group as they sneaked off the beautiful, pristine campus in Annapolis, Maryland, to a seedy nearby bar. When the shore patrol caught them in the unauthorized bar most of the midshipman were able to escape out a back door. McCain was caught and driven back to the Academy by the laughing shore patrol officers.

The worst aspect of McCain's years at Annapolis was his company captain. The captain made no secret of the fact he thought McCain had made it into the Academy because he was the scion of a naval family. He made it his task to drive McCain out of the Academy before he graduated.

The captain was continuously looking for opportunities to have McCain expelled. Shortly before McCain's graduation he made one last attempt. He performed a surprise inspection of McCain's room and judged it to be in "gross disorder." The customary penalty for the infraction, according to McCain, was fifteen demerits. The captain gave McCain seventy-five. This put McCain so close to the 125 limit it was tantamount to expulsion.

McCain reacted immediately to what he saw as outright unfairness. He decided to leave the Academy before he was kicked out and telephoned his parents and told them of his decision. They asked him to wait and not make a hasty decision.

A few days later McCain received a summons to go see the Commandant of the Naval Academy. The Commandant asked him why he was leaving. McCain answered that he had too many demerits.

McCain then complained that he had been unfairly punished by his captain. The Commandant agreed that he had not been treated fairly and agreed to reduce his demerits so he could graduate. He then went on to say that McCain was spoiled. McCain didn't disagree, but claimed that it still wasn't fair.

Despite his behavior record, McCain excelled at some tasks. The summer between the third and last year every midshipman was required to make his first voyage on a naval ship. McCain's assignment was to sail to Rio de Janeiro.

President Eisenhower spoke during the graduation ceremony for McCain's Naval Academy class.

McCain excelled on this first naval assignment. He liked the ship's captain and responded well to his gruff demeanor. McCain discovered that he was good at handling the ship and almost perfectly executed a difficult maneuver in pulling up beside a refueling ship.

While in Rio de Janeiro, McCain had a short-term, intense affair with a Brazilian fashion model. He met her at a party and the two were almost inseparable until McCain returned to Annapolis.

A young McCain (left) stands beside his mother and father during the dedication of McCain Field, a U.S. Navy training base. *(Courtesy of AP Images)*

President Eisenhower spoke at the graduation ceremony for the class of 1958. Midshipman McCain graduated fifth from the bottom, but he graduated. Although he would later say that he hated every minute he was at the Naval Academy, he also acknowledged that it helped to prepare him for the travails he would face during his years in the military. He had embarked on a journey that would take him to a bloody war, the hell of a North Vietnamese prison camp, and eventually to the brink of the highest office of the country his family had served proudly for generations.

two
Fire!

When McCain graduated from the Naval Academy in the spring of 1958, the U.S. had only a few dozen military and political advisers in South Vietnam. Vietnam had been controlled by France for most of the twentieth century and was known, along with other countries in Southeast Asia, as French Indochina. When World War II ended, France was exhausted, and colonialism was out of favor. Taking advantage of the situation, the Vietnamese people rose in rebellion and eventually drove the French out in 1954.

Ho Chi Minh

The conflict in Vietnam did not stop after the French left. There was a deep division between the northern part of the country and the south. Centered on the capital of Hanoi, the north was under the control of Ho Chi Minh and his supporters, who had committed to the development of a Communist society and received aid from the Soviet Union. The leaders in the south resisted becoming Communist and looked to western nations to help.

Vietnam

An open conflict between the north and south was avoided for a few years after each side agreed to stay on their side of the thirteenth parallel. Elections were planned for 1956 across the entire country so the people could decide on unification and how Vietnam should be governed. But the elections were never held and Vietnam slipped into a complicated, terribly bloody war.

The U.S. was locked into the Cold War with the Soviet Union, and was committed to stopping the expansion of communism. By the end of the 1950s, Vietnam had become the front of this global conflict. However, U.S. involvement happened gradually for almost a decade. Then in August 1964, in reaction to an attack against U.S. ships in the Tonkin Gulf of Vietnam, Congress granted President Lyndon Johnson unlimited authority to escalate U.S. involvement in the war in Vietnam. By the spring of 1965, more than 100,000 American troops had been sent to the jungles of Vietnam, and thousands more would be sent before the U.S. pulled out in 1973.

Vietnam was just one of many tense spots on the globe when McCain left Annapolis. It would be almost a decade before he was sent to fly bombing missions over Hanoi. Meanwhile, he had to learn to fly.

In August 1958, McCain reported to the navy's flight training school in Pensacola, Florida. He had decided to become a naval pilot and learn how to fly and land on aircraft carriers. He remained in Pensacola for two and a half years. While there he learned to fly, and he continued to build his reputation as an irreverent and somewhat irresponsible young man. In navy parlance, John McCain was a "cowboy." He went to nightclubs whenever possible and dated a seemingly endless string of local women from all walks of life. One night he took an exotic dancer to a formal dinner party with fellow—and superior—officers and their wives.

McCain soon learned that flying was highly risky. On one training flight out of Texas, his engine died and he crashed into the Gulf of Mexico. He was knocked unconscious and almost drowned before coming to. The next night he went out and partied.

McCain had his first brush with war in October 1962. Early in the month U.S. spy planes sighted nuclear silo missiles and other evidence that the Soviets were installing nuclear weapons on the island nation Cuba, ninety miles off the Florida coast. Cuba had recently come under the control of Fidel Castro, a Communist and ally of the Soviet Union.

President Kennedy warned Soviet leader Nikita Khrushchev to remove the missiles or the U.S. would have no choice but to retaliate—with nuclear weapons if necessary. At first

Khrushchev rejected Kennedy's demands, and tensions rose. McCain and dozens of other navy and air force pilots were ordered to begin flying over Cuba. After a few tense days Khrushchev announced he would remove the missiles, and the crisis ended.

McCain spent the first half of the 1960s moving from base to base. But he was never out of danger. In the fall of 1965 he crashed another plane while landing at a base outside of Norfolk, Virginia. He had to eject from the plane only seconds before it slammed into some trees. McCain seemed to relish his reputation as a cowboy, but those around him noticed that he was slowly beginning to calm down. As he admitted later, near death events helped him to reevaluate what his life should be about.

His desire to settle down only increased when he fell in love and became a husband and father. McCain had known

Lieutenant John McCain (bottom right) in 1965 *(Courtesy of Corbis)*

The U.S.S. *Forrestal*

Carol Shepp when he was at Annapolis; she had dated a fellow midshipman. She had married the midshipman and had two children, but when McCain ran into her again she was divorced. She and McCain began dating and were married in the summer of 1965. McCain later adopted her two sons, and they had a daughter, Sidney, in 1966.

By the time McCain was married, the Vietnam War had become the focus of U.S. foreign and military policy. In the fall of 1966, he began asking to be sent to Vietnam. In the spring of 1967 he got his wish and was assigned to the U.S.S. *Forrestal*, an aircraft carrier patrolling of the coast of North Vietnam. McCain made bombing runs off the *Forrestal* in an A-4 Skyhawk, a light bomber and fighter plane.

By July 29, 1967, he had flown five missions. That morning he stepped onto the flight deck for his sixth run. He ran through his preflight procedures and climbed into the cockpit to prepare for takeoff.

As he climbed into the Skyhawk, a nearby fighter plane, an F-4 Phantom, accidentally fired a Zuni missile. It tore through McCain's external fuel tank, and his A-4 Skyhawk was driven across the flight deck as the fuel streamed out of the ruptured tank.

The spilled fuel was ablaze in an instant; flames rushed across the deck. McCain climbed out of the cockpit when his plane stopped its skid. Just as he had escaped, the A-4 exploded. The entire flight deck all around him was burning. He had no choice but to jump into the flames and roll. Parts of his flight suit were set on fire.

Crew members fight the fires aboard the U.S.S. *Forrestal* following explosions from an accidental missile deployment. *(Courtesy of the Naval Historical Center)*

McCain finally got to his feet and began to run from the flames. Suddenly, another Skyhawk exploded behind him, killing the pilot and three other sailors. McCain was again knocked off his feet.

More planes and bombs began exploding across the entire deck. Men desperately began pushing planes into the ocean to keep them from exploding. They unloaded bomb bays and tossed the missiles overboard.

McCain was wounded and burned, but escaped serious injury. He was lucky. It took hours to bring the fire under control and before it was over 134 men were dead. The total damages were more than $100 million. The carrier was barely able to make its way to a naval base in the Philippines and was out of commission for two years.

For the third time, McCain had survived a brush with death. It seemed that he was charmed somehow. Days after the tragedy he began looking for a new carrier to be assigned to—he was anxious to get back to flying bombing missions over North Vietnam.

three
POW

After the fire on the *Forrestal*, McCain looked for another carrier to fly off. When he learned that the *Oriskany* needed pilots, he signed up. He was warned that the *Oriskany* had lost more pilots than any other carrier, but McCain brushed off the warnings. He had already escaped death three times since becoming a pilot. Maybe he was destined for something big.

After a leave traveling with his family in Europe, McCain returned to the waters near Vietnam in September 1967. As he was leaving he told Carol and his children that he should be home by summer.

McCain's first missions off the *Oriskany* were successful. President Lyndon B. Johnson had lifted many of the restrictions that had been imposed on which targets could be bombed. He had been concerned that if facilities manned by the Soviet Union were destroyed the conflict could explode into a global, nuclear confrontation. But the war was becoming unpopular at home and Johnson had decided to try to bring it to a quick, successful conclusion. McCain and the other pilots were enthusiastic that the restrictions had been lifted. They had been frustrated at what they saw as political interference in the war. Now they could take the fight to the enemy.

McCain was flying an A-4 Skyhawk, used mostly for light bombing off aircraft carriers. It was small and more easily maneuverable than earlier attack planes, but several had been shot down by Surface to Air Missiles (SAMs) that the Soviet Union had given to their North Vietnamese allies. Pilots described the SAMs as looking like telephone poles zooming toward them

As McCain prepared to fly out that morning the deck officer warned him to take extra caution. The North Vietnamese were certain to be ready for more bombings. McCain, always the brash, confident one, responded, "You don't have to worry about me."

McCain's mission that day was to destroy a power plant near Hanoi. To reach his goal he had to fly over the heavily fortified city. The North Vietnamese were desperate to protect the plant. As he approached McCain took evasive action to avoid being hit. He went into a dive and swooped over the plant and released his bombs—but as he began to pull out of the dive a missile took off his right wing.

Suddenly the Skyhawk was spiraling toward the ground. McCain pulled his ejection toggle cord. The sudden force of the ejection rockets broke his arms; his right knee was shattered when it smashed into the instrument panel.

The force also knocked him unconscious momentarily. He came to when his plane exploded on impact. He had just enough time to see he was falling into a shallow body of water located in the middle of Hanoi. He learned later the water was called Truc Bach (White Bamboo) Lake.

McCain was wearing fifty pounds of equipment when he hit the lake—and his arms and one leg were broken. He sank to the bottom and desperately tried to swim to the top, but was only able to bop up long enough to gasp a lungful of air before sinking again. Finally, he was able to use his teeth to pull the toggle cord on his inflatable life vest and float to the surface.

A large, excited crowd gathered around the lake's shore. The citizens of Hanoi had suffered days of bombing and were angry. Some men from the crowd swam out and pulled McCain to shore, where the crowd stripped him of his uniform and equipment. Then, as he rolled on the ground trying to push himself up with is broken arms and leg, the crowd began kicking and pounding him with their fists, spitting and yelling the entire time. Someone drove a bayonet into

McCain is rescued from Hanoi's Truc Bach lake by local citizens after his plane was shot down by North Vietnamese forces. *(Courtesy of AFP/ Getty Images)*

An aerial view of Hoa Loa prison

his leg and groin. Another drove his rifle butt into his shoulder and broke it. He howled with pain. Finally, a man and woman drove the crowd back and protected McCain until soldiers arrived.

McCain was tossed into the back of a truck and taken to the prison that Americans had dubbed the Hanoi Hilton, one of a series of POW prisons in Hanoi. The prison's official name was Hoa Loa.

Initially, McCain was bandaged and left on the floor of a cell. His captors insisted he must divulge everything he knew about U.S. forces or plans before he would be treated for his life-threatening wounds. McCain refused, giving only his name, rank, serial number, and date of birth.

Over the next days McCain received only small amounts of food and water. The other captives who saw him assumed he would be dead within the week. He was unconscious much of the time and couldn't keep the little bit of food he was given down. His wounds were soon infected and his captors did

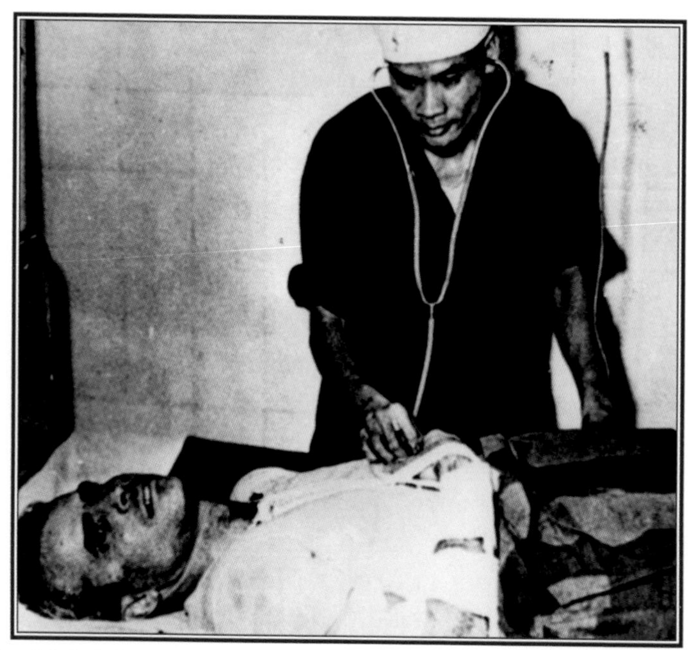

After McCain's captors learned he was the son of Admiral Jack McCain, they took him to a hospital and began treating his injuries. *(Courtesy of AP Images)*

nothing to keep the infection from spreading. But McCain persisted in his refusal to be interrogated.

McCain would have probably died if the North Vietnamese did not learn that he was the son of an admiral. When they learned that Jack McCain was his father they began to show more interest in his welfare. McCain could be a valuable propaganda tool, especially if they could get him to confess to war crimes or speak out against U.S. involvement in the war.

Earlier, when a doctor had visited him he had pronounced that it was too late; there was nothing he could do. McCain would die regardless of any treatment they could give him. McCain begged to be taken to a hospital. Even when he said, "Take me to the hospital and I'll give you the information you want," the doctor refused.

After his identity was revealed, McCain was taken to a hospital, where he was given much needed blood and some antibiotics to quell the infection. Then he was left untreated.

After two weeks, McCain was moved and a doctor made an effort to set some of his broken bones. Without giving him anything for pain, or knocking him out with anesthesia, the doctor worked on his right arm for over two hours before giving up. He then wrapped his body in a plaster cast from the waist to his neck. The broken, unset arm was wrapped so that it protruded above his head and he was left alone in his hospital room.

A few hours after the cast was put on it became clear why his captors had tried to make it look as though he had been well treated. He was informed that a French television crew was at the prison and they wanted to interview

McCain received substandard medical care during his time as a POW, and his broken arms were allowed to heal without being properly set. *(Courtesy of AP Images)*

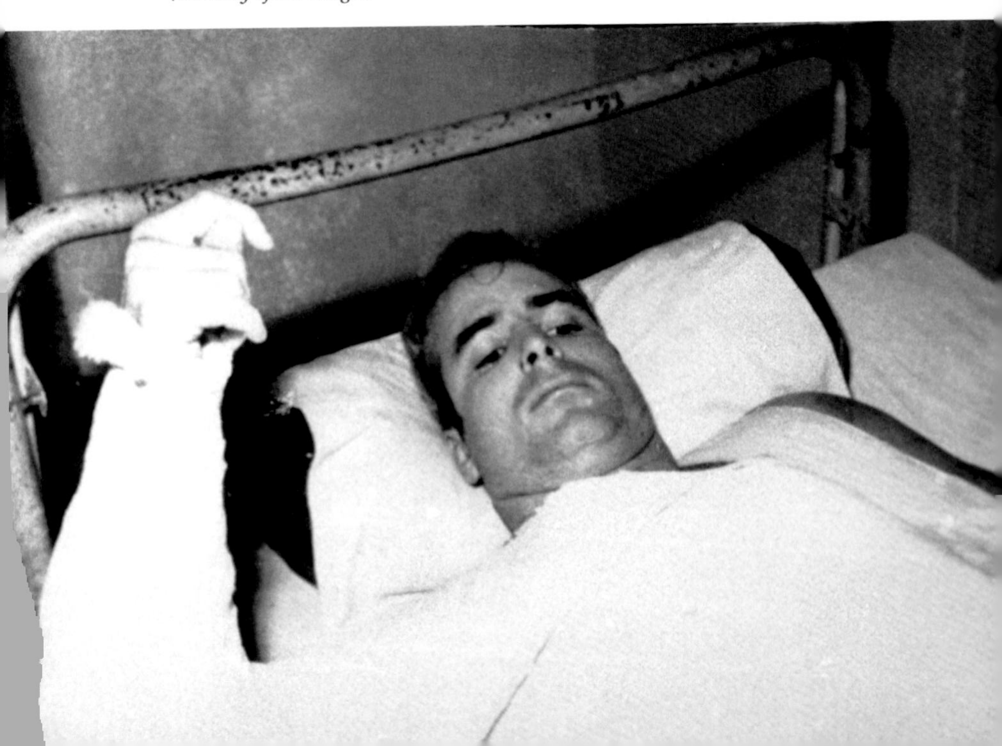

McCain. McCain wanted his family to know he was alive, but the North Vietnamese wanted him to say he had received humane treatment, and to ask the U.S. government to withdraw from Vietnam to stop killing innocent people. McCain agreed, but during the interview he refused to say what his captors wanted him to say. After the camera crew was gone his infuriated captors took him back to his hospital room and kicked and punched him until his screams echoed down the hallways.

The work that was done on McCain's injuries might have been worse than leaving them unattended. The doctors treated his broken knee by cutting the ligaments and cartilage, and his arms were allowed to knit back without being properly reset, leaving him unable to raise his arms above his head. Today, he cannot comb his own hair and still walks with a limp.

Although the guards and other prison officials seemed to be indifferent about McCain's survival, he came to realize he was more valuable to them alive than dead. Although he didn't know it at the time, his father had been transferred from Europe and made commander-in-chief of all military forces in the Pacific, including Vietnam, making John McCain a very high level prisoner.

The North Vietnamese decided that the best way to use McCain's status would be to convince him to take an early release. The Code of Military Conduct establishes strict rules governing the timing of the release of POWs. The rule was that the men should be released in the order they were captured; the longest serving should go first. There where several POWs who had been held longer than McCain.

McCain refused early release. The offer was tempting. "I wanted to say yes," he said. "I badly wanted to go home."

He suffered from his wounds, as well as dysentery and other ailments throughout captivity. But he knew if he left it would be a propaganda victory for the North Vietnamese, as well as disloyal to his fellow prisoners. He refused the offer. Even when they told him President Johnson had approved his release, and that his injuries provided him an exception to the Code of Conduct rule, McCain refused.

McCain was again kicked and beaten. The North Vietnamese changed their tactics and told him he had been judged as a war criminal and would be tried and executed. They insisted he make a taped confession of the crimes he had committed against the North Vietnamese people. McCain refused.

The guards, determined to break the admiral's son, began their most brutal torture. They removed his cast and cinched his broken arms behind his back with what were called torture ropes and left him sitting on a stool for hours. The pain was excruciating. When he continued to refuse to "confess," they beat him mercilessly.

Over the next days they continued to torture McCain with the ropes and beatings. When he could no longer sit on the stool and fell to the floor he was left to wallow in his own waste.

After a week of this treatment McCain agreed to do what they asked. They took him into a room and forced him to write down all the war crimes he had committed. McCain tried to sabotage the report by making obvious errors that he hoped would indicate he was only writing the report under duress.

After writing the report, although he only did it after terrible torture, McCain was desolate. He felt he had brought dishonor on himself, his country, and his family. He even made an attempt at suicide, but was stopped before he could carry it out. His captors beat him for attempting to take his own life. McCain's feelings of shame at breaking under torture have haunted him ever since.

Even the forced confession did not stop the beatings and mistreatment. He was left in solitary confinement until December 1970. In all, he spent more than three years in solitary.

After his release from solitary, the conditions improved. McCain was housed with a large group of other American prisoners. The men developed various ways to make the time pass. They retold the plots of movies they had seen and played memory games. They held church services, despite the rules against practicing religion in the officially atheistic North Vietnam.

The POWs were especially pleased when the Americans began bombing Hanoi again in 1972. The bombings had been called off while representatives from the U.S. and North Vietnam held peace talks in Paris. When the talks broke down, President Nixon ordered a renewal of the bombings, in hopes of breaking the diplomatic impasse.

Eventually, the peace talks resumed and finally bore fruit in January 1973. The U.S. agreed to withdraw its troops from Vietnam. One of the other terms of the agreement was that all the POWs would be released.

The Paris agreement went into effect on January 28. Afterward, the POWs were released in groups, the longest serving leaving first. The first group left Hanoi on February 12. McCain boarded a plane on March 14. He had been in captivity for six years.

The war between North and South Vietnam continued for two more years. Finally, after the U.S. Congress cut off

McCain is escorted to a Hanoi airport by a public relations officer after being released from Hoa Loa prison. *(Courtesy of AP Images)*

most of the aid to South Vietnam, regular troops from North Vietnam rolled into the South Vietnamese capital of Saigon (now known as Ho Chi Minh City.) The long war was over and the South Vietnamese allies of the U.S. had lost. McCain swore that if he had anything to say about it the U.S. would never again send troops to a war without having the full support of the American people.

four

From Hanoi to Congress

After his release, McCain was flown to Clark Air Force Base in the Philippines. There he learned that his wife Carol had been in a terrible car accident on Christmas Eve of 1969. She had been thrown from her car. In the hospital her left leg was so badly damaged the doctors considered amputating. She also had severe internal injuries and was on the verge of death for several days. She had gone through two years of physical therapy and was confined to a wheelchair and crutches. When her treatment was over she was four inches shorter than before the accident.

When Carol told him about her accident in a telephone conversation while he was still in the Philippines she warned him that she looked much different than she had before McCain left for Vietnam. "Well, you know, I don't look so good myself," he said.

McCain landed in Jacksonville, Florida, where his family was living, on St. Patrick's Day. He was on crutches when

McCain stands with his first wife, Carol, shortly after his arrival in the U.S. after spending six years in a North Vietnamese POW camp. *(Courtesy of AP Images)*

he disembarked from the plane to be greeted by Carol and his children. It was his first time seeing them in more than six years.

The son of an admiral, McCain received more press attention than most of the other returning POWs. Even after the fanfare ended, he was sought out by reporters and received requests to speak before the Veterans of Foreign Wars and other organizations. He also began writing articles, usually for the national news weekly *U.S. News and World Report* detailing life inside the North Vietnamese prison.

President Nixon, who was in the midst of the Watergate Scandal that would eventually drive him from office in August 1974, hosted a dinner and reception for the returning POWs at the White House. McCain was one of the most sought out of the honored guests.

McCain attends a White House reception for returning POWs, hosted by President Nixon (left). *(Courtesy of AP Images)*

When he returned home McCain planned to stay in the navy. But if he wanted to fly again he needed to become flexible enough to again qualify as a pilot. Because of his injuries he might not be able to operate the controls, or to eject if there was another crash.

McCain worked with a physical therapist to restore flexibility to his knee. Through daily, excruciatingly painful sessions he was finally able to bend his knee enough to meet pilot qualifications. Over the next years McCain had a variety of postings. He was not the same cowboy pilot he had been before Vietnam and seemed to be taking his career more seriously.

McCain was a student for a year at the Naval War College in Washington, D.C., while he was undergoing physical therapy.

He studied military strategy, and how politics and strategy intersected. He was beginning to become more interested in how political leaders made decisions during war time.

After leaving the war college, and finishing his physical therapy, he was sent back to Jacksonville to command a group that trained pilots. Although he had never had a command position before, McCain rose to the challenge. He had a crew of over a thousand men, as well as seventy-five planes under his command. The training group had received mediocre reviews before McCain took charge. Before he left it was receiving top reviews and McCain was praised for his exceptional leadership.

McCain tried to arrange a trip to tour Vietnam, although he had only been home a short while. He was not able to get permission from Hanoi to return. He was determined to return some day. He was clearly trying to come to terms with all aspects of the Vietnam War: what policy decisions were responsible for the escalation of U.S. involvement; why were the North Vietnamese and their Vietcong allies in the south more determined to win; most critically, why had so many Americans turned against the war?

McCain's thinking and studying was moving him closer and closer to politics. He was still a naval officer but was beginning to question if he wanted to remain in the navy. It became clear he would never become a full admiral like his father and grandfather. If he stayed in the navy there would be a ceiling on his ambitions.

Meanwhile, he had another crisis to face. When he first came home from Hanoi he and Carol bought a beach house and even thought of having another child. But over the next few years they began to grow apart. He later confessed to being unfaithful during this period and finding it difficult to return his marriage to what it was in 1967. After a series of separations and reconciliations, he and Carol separated for good. They would finalize their divorce in 1980.

McCain's last naval assignment was as a liaison officer between the navy and the U.S. Senate. His job was to coordinate relationships and logistics between senators and the navy. He was the person senators called when one of his or her constituents had trouble receiving treatment at a hospital or a disability check was held up.

The job brought McCain into contact with powerful senators from both the Democratic and Republican parties. He had grown up around politicians. As a high-ranking naval officer stationed in Washington off and on during his career, his father had entertained well-known politicians in his home. But this was the first time McCain had worked closely with senators who voted on military budgets and made other decisions important to all four branches of the military.

McCain befriended senators from both parties. Two who became particularly close were William Cohen, Republican from Maine, and Gary Hart, Democrat from Colorado. Cohen would later become Defense Secretary under Democratic President Bill Clinton, and Gary Hart would run for president in 1984 and 1988. Both men were active in the movement to use the bitter lessons learned from the Vietnam War to reform the military.

The three men shared many of the same ideas about how the U.S. should approach the rest of the world. They discussed other issues and socialized. All were approximately the same age and liked to find ways to relax in Washington or while on foreign trips.

One of McCain's duties was to travel with senators when they visited other countries. If any of the discussions a senator was going to have with foreign leaders involved the navy, or U.S. policy that involved the navy, McCain was required to travel as the eyes and ears of the navy, and to offer advice when it was requested. McCain was popular with most senators and they enjoyed having him accompany them.

Occasionally, on evenings after the work was done, the old McCain would emerge. He was single again and saw no reason why he shouldn't go out to clubs—if any were available. One of his tasks in Islamic countries, where alcohol was forbidden, was to smuggle enough whiskey into a senator's room for him to have a nightcap.

There was some fun in being the navy liaison officer, but there was a great deal of work to be done. Jimmy Carter was president and the country was still reeling from the loss of Vietnam. There was a strong consensus to decrease military spending and to cancel some weapon systems, ships, and aircraft that were either in the developmental stage or had already been ordered. McCain considered his chief accomplishment as the liaison officer was to make sure the navy got a new aircraft carrier that President Carter wanted to cancel.

During this time McCain's political ideology became more firm. He had long been a committed Republican, although he was not afraid to disagree with his party on some policies. As the 1980 presidential campaign warmed up he was an early supporter of former California governor Ronald Reagan. He had met Reagan soon after his homecoming, and was impressed by his personality and his commitment to a strong national defense. After the military defeat, economic downturn, political corruption, and the split in America over several other divisive issues that had occurred over the last fifteen years, McCain thought that Reagan's confident belief in his own ideas was what the country needed.

McCain also came to a final decision about his future that year. He went to his father and broke the news that he was retiring from the navy. He would never achieve the high rank his father, and grandfather, had attained and his heart was no longer into it. He wanted to enter politics. Although Jack McCain did not deny he was disappointed about the decision, he told his son he understood and gave him his blessing. Jack McCain died soon after, in March 1981. McCain officially resigned from the navy only days later.

McCain was determined to run for Congress. Although he had lived in Florida longer than any other state, he had another state in mind that he thought would provide him a better opportunity. There was also another reason to relocate.

McCain had met Cindy Hensley at a formal reception in Honolulu, Hawaii, in the winter of 1979, while he was still working in Washington. At the time she was the twenty-five-year-old daughter of one of the wealthiest men in Arizona. The Hensley family owned the largest beer distributor in the state.

From the first moment he met Cindy, McCain was smitten. They began dating, although she lived in Arizona and he was in Washington. They were married in May 1980, soon after his divorce from Carol became final.

The couple was married in Phoenix, Arizona. McCain had already decided to leave the navy by that point and Arizona offered him the best chance of any state to begin a political career. He had never lived there before and knew

McCain and his second wife, Cindy, attend a military ball in this 2006 photo. *(Courtesy of the U.S. Department of Defense)*

few people, but Cindy's family was influential and helped him to meet important people. Her father was well known in Republican circles.

Another advantage to Arizona was that the majority of its citizens had relocated there from somewhere else. The population had boomed in recent years. It was an attractive place for retirees and thousands of older voters who had escaped the colder northern states for the warm desert. Others had moved there for better opportunities.

McCain had never lived in any state for a long period of time. He had grown up in the navy moving from posting to posting as a child and as an adult. But he knew he would nevertheless be open to charges of being a "carpetbagger," someone who had only come to the state to run for office, when he entered politics in Arizona. But it would be a charge he would have to face anywhere, and it was probably the best state to deal with the issue.

McCain moved to Tempe, Arizona, where he went to work for Cindy's father. Everyone in the family knew he wanted to enter politics and the job was temporary. His job was in public relations, which allowed him to speak before civic groups and other influential groups, and to meet possible contributors.

Initially, McCain thought he would have to wait several years before a seat would come open. Arizona was a heavily Republican state and there were few signs one of the incumbent representatives intended to retire. Then a powerful congressman, former minority leader John Rhodes, of the First Congressional District, announced he would not seek reelection in 1982. Suddenly, McCain had an opening.

There was one problem. McCain didn't live in the First District. But this problem was quickly solved. Cindy simply bought a house in the district. McCain later admitted that there were certain advantages to entering politics with a wealthy spouse.

The First Congressional District of Arizona

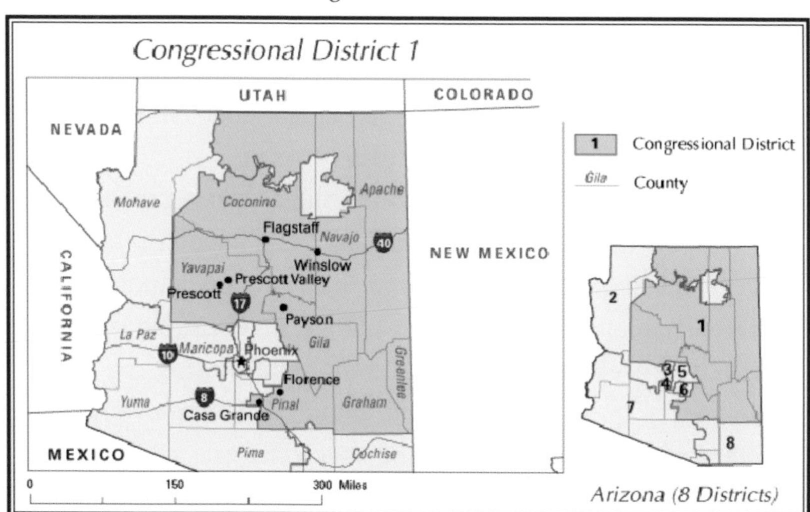

McCain immediately began campaigning. He and Cindy traveled the district, speaking before groups and shaking hands. A political consultant advised McCain that his biggest challenge was to become known to the voters and told him to go door-to-door and simply introduce himself and say he was running for Congress. Throughout the winter, spring, and into the blistering desert summer, McCain and a campaign aid walked the sidewalks of the sections of Tempe, Phoenix, and other areas in the district.

The critical race was for the Republican nomination. The district was so heavily Republican a Democratic candidate had little chance of winning in the general election. Several Republicans entered the race. McCain started out last in the polls. He was a recent transplant to the state and his opponents had served in state and local offices.

McCain was undeterred and continued working twelve to eighteen hours everyday. Cindy worked almost as hard. They raised money via the telephone to fund his campaign and attended fundraisers organized by Cindy and her father.

When McCain began moving up in the polls the other candidates took notice, and the inevitable attacks that he was a carpetbagger began. It was the biggest obstacle he faced, and he struggled for a way to overcome it.

He finally got the chance to put the carpetbagger charge to rest during a candidate's debate. The race was almost over, and he had developed into the strongest candidate. It had been a long, hard race and, as McCain admitted later, he was tired of the campaign and even more tired of the other candidates questioning how he could understand Arizona voters when he had lived in the state only one year. In this debate he finally snapped and ignored his advisers' pleas to control his temper. After a candidate repeatedly brought up the charge, McCain responded. "Listen pal," he said, "I wish I could have had the luxury, like you, of growing up and living and spending my entire life in a nice place like the first district of Arizona, but I was doing other things. As a matter of fact, when I think about it now, the place I lived the longest in my life was Hanoi."

After a moment of stunned silence the audience burst into applause. The debate was essentially over, and according to the recollections of McCain and others who witnessed the debate, so was the campaign. McCain went on to win a majority of the vote in a four-person race.

As expected McCain handily beat his Democratic opponent in November. In January 1982, John McCain was back in Washington. This time he was a congressman in his own right. But his ambition was not satisfied. He was already thinking of moving up to the U.S. Senate.

five
Ascent

In many ways, McCain's return to Washington was a homecoming. Most of the people he had known as a naval liaison were senators, but he had met a number of U.S. Representatives as well. His good friends William Cohen and Gary Hart were still in the Senate and they often socialized together and attended the same events.

McCain needed the companionship, as his wife Cindy had stayed in Arizona. To help counteract the carpetbagger charge, McCain had promised the voters of the First District that he would return home every weekend. It was a heavy burden to fly back and forth across the country each week, but he kept his promise. Cindy staying in Arizona was smart politically and personally. They wanted to start a family, and Cindy wanted her children to grow up in her beloved Arizona.

Ronald Reagan had been elected president in 1980 and had come into office promising to make many changes, including lowering taxes and cutting federal spending. He promised to present a tough, even aggressive, face to the world—particularly to the Soviet Union. The U.S. and the Soviet Union were still locked in the Cold War that had begun soon after World War II. Reagan wanted to make the Soviet Union aware that, despite the loss in Vietnam, the U.S. was determined to prevail.

McCain had long been a supporter of Reagan, who came to political prominence during the 1960s. Reagan had advocated a more aggressive military policy in Vietnam. Word of Reagan's speeches had occasionally leaked into the Vietnamese prisons, and McCain, along with most of the POWs, had agreed with what Reagan said.

Although McCain supported and admired Reagan, he found himself disagreeing with him soon after he came to Washington. The disagreement was over Middle East policy.

The country of Lebanon was being ripped apart by a bloody civil war and had been invaded by the neighboring countries of Syria and Israel. As the central government collapsed under the pressure and the violence escalated and threatened to spill over into other countries, the Reagan administration decided to send troops to try to establish and maintain a ceasefire.

The president asked Congress for permission to send U.S. marines to Lebanon. The vast majority of McCain's Republican colleagues supported sending the marines, but McCain was opposed. He thought it was another example of U.S. political leaders using military forces carelessly. The situation in Lebanon was extremely chaotic and combustible, he argued, and a few hundred U.S. marines would make no

Smoke rises from the U.S. Marine barracks in Lebanon after the October 23, 1983, suicide bombing. *(Courtesy of the U.S. Marine Corps)*

difference. Even worse, they would instantly become targets of terrorist attacks.

McCain lost on the vote, but tragically he turned out to be right. A few weeks after the marines arrived in Lebanon, on October 23, 1983, a suicide bomber drove a truck loaded with explosives into the marine barracks, killing 314 U.S. marines. Four days later, Reagan announced he was pulling out the rest of the troops.

Despite his unwillingness to go along with his party when its policies violated his own conscience, McCain was popular with his colleagues. They even voted him president of the freshman class of Republicans, an honorary title.

McCain's hard work taking care of his constituents' needs, and his exhausting policy of going home every weekend, solidified his hold on the First District of Arizona. He was also popular for supporting President Reagan on most issues. He easily won reelection in 1984.

Only a few weeks after he was reelected, McCain received a telephone call from Walter Cronkite, the legendary CBS reporter and news anchor. Cronkite was calling to ask McCain to travel with him and a news crew to Vietnam. McCain had already tried once to go back to Vietnam but had been denied a visa by the Communist government. He jumped at the chance to go this time.

Cronkite was making a documentary about Vietnam ten years after the war ended and the Communists took over. He was sure he could get McCain a visa, but that turned out to harder than he expected.

McCain publicly announced that while in Vietnam he would bring up the burning issue of the Missing In Action (MIAs). The MIA issue was a major concern for McCain and many other veterans and their families in the years after the war. More than 2,000 U.S. troops were unaccounted for at war's end. Their bodies had not been recovered. There was no certain evidence any of them had survived, but some MIA advocate groups, and dozens of families of the missing Americans, were

Walter Cronkite *(Courtesy of AP Images/Scott Applewhite)*

convinced there were still prisoners being held in Vietnam. The government of Vietnam insisted they had released all the POWs and that the missing had been killed and their bodies lost in the vast jungles or elsewhere.

The MIA issue would later become a point of contention between McCain and some of the more militant veteran's groups, and would help to sabotage his 2000 presidential campaign. But in 1985 he was solidly behind the drive to find out what had happened to the missing Americans.

After McCain brought up the MIA issue, the Vietnamese government denied him a visa. Undeterred, McCain traveled to nearby Bangkok, Thailand, as a way to pressure the government to grant him entry. After four futile days McCain flew home to be with Cindy when she gave birth to their first child, Meghan. He and Cindy would eventually have three children.

A month later the Vietnamese government relented and granted him a visa. McCain and the CBS crew were going to Hanoi. McCain showed Cronkite and millions of U.S. viewers Truc Bach Lake. As they stood at the lake a crowd of people gathered around and shook McCain's hand. He learned that he was famous in Hanoi. He even joked that in Vietnam he was more famous than Cronkite.

They visited the prison where McCain had spent time and been tortured. They toured the cells and McCain related incidents that had occurred during his captivity.

The program, *Honor, Duty, and a War Called Vietnam* aired on CBS and was well received. McCain's courage in returning, and his mostly calm demeanor as he showed Cronkite and the American audience the places where he had suffered torture and lived in almost constant fear for his life,

In this 1985 photo, McCain holds a picture of the monument on the shore of Truc Bach Lake that marks the site of his rescue. *(Courtesy of AP Images/Jim Bourdier)*

dramatically heightened his reputation. Politically, it was more valuable than millions of dollars of television ads.

McCain would soon put the positive publicity to good use. Longtime Arizona senator Barry Goldwater, 1964 Republican presidential candidate and the man credited with founding the modern conservative movement, announced he would not run for reelection in 1986.

McCain had planned ever since he entered politics to run for the U.S. Senate at the first opportunity. Now he had the opportunity.

The 1986 Senate race looked like it was going to be a battle of the titans of Arizona politics. Although the state was heavily Republican, it had a Democratic governor, Bruce Babbit, who was very popular. The son of a prominent Arizona family, Babbit was not easily identified with the "Eastern liberal" wing of his party. He also had a record as a good steward of the economy, which appealed to the growing conservation movement. Babbit would have been a formidable challenger to McCain, but he decided not to run for Senate and to instead enter the 1988 presidential race, where he was not successful.

Babbit's decision not to run made it easier for McCain, but he again had to deal with the carpetbagger charge—this time in a statewide race. The charge had less impact than before, however, because he had served two terms in the House of Representatives and had developed a reputation as a hard-working congressman whose views were usually in line with most Arizona voters.

Republicans had controlled the Senate since 1980, but after the 1986 votes were tallied they had lost control of the Senate and lost seats in the House of Representatives. McCain easily won his seat, as was expected, but he entered the Senate in the minority. This meant he would not get to chair any committees or control any of the agenda.

Soon after he was sworn in as a senator in 1987, McCain ran into one of the biggest controversies of the decade: The Iran-Contra Affair. For a while, this scandal even threatened to bring down the presidency of Ronald Reagan and involved two of the most divisive foreign policy issues of the 1980s.

Relations with the nation of Iran had been tense since 1978. That year the U.S.-backed government of the shah of Iran was toppled by a revolt led by the Ayatollah Khomeini and other Shiite Muslim clerics. The shah was accused of controlling Iran by the brutal use of secret police, and the new leaders held the U.S. responsible for supporting the shah. They also charged most of the West of being decadent and of spreading immoral values throughout the world.

In 1979, Iranian students took over the U.S. embassy in Iran's capital city of Tehran and took sixty-six employees hostage. The Iranian hostage crisis continued until the day Reagan was inaugurated, January 20, 1981, when the hostages were released.

Although the hostages were released, tension between the U.S. and Iran continued to escalate. Iran was accused of backing terrorist groups and supporting the kidnappings of Americans in Lebanon. The U.S. cut off all diplomatic relations with the country and made it illegal to sell weapons to the Iranian government.

The other hotly contested foreign policy issue of the time involved anti-government rebels in Nicaragua. The rebels, called contras, were opposed to the pro-Communist Sandinista government in Nicaragua. The Reagan administration and many Republicans in Congress wanted to provide financial and military support to the contras, but most Democrats were opposed. The Democrats controlled Congress and were able to pass laws forbidding the U.S. from aiding the contras.

These two foreign policy issues came together in the Iran-Contra Affair. Beginning in 1985, officials in the Reagan Administration secretly sold weapons to the Iranians in hopes of getting Iranian help in freeing American hostages held in Lebanon. The money from the arm sales was then used secretly to fund the contras in Nicaragua.

When the elaborate plan was uncovered in November 1986, it became the biggest political scandal of the decade. President

Reagan initially said he knew nothing about the arm sales but later had to admit he had been briefed.

During the Iran-Contra Affair, U.S. weapons were sold to Iran to fund the contra rebel movement in Nicaragua. *(Courtesy of AP Images/ Iran-Contra Committee HO)*

National Security Advisor John Poindexter had to resign and was charged with criminal wrongdoing. He had been a classmate of McCain's at the Naval Academy. McCain tried to convince his old classmate to testify openly and honestly before the congressional committees investigating the matter, but Poindexter refused.

The Iran-Contra Affair dragged on for the remainder of Reagan's presidency. McCain publicly supported the president's effort to aid the contras. He agreed that the Sandinista government should be replaced and was convinced it was trying to spread communism in the hemisphere. But he also publicly criticized the arms sales to Iran and spoke out against the members of the Reagan administration who refused to answer questions.

McCain's attitude toward the Iran-Contra Affair ended up antagonizing some of his Republican colleagues. It was clear that he would not support members of his party he thought might have committed crimes or had lied to Congress. Many other Republicans thought the right thing to do was always speak out for fellow party members. McCain's willingness to follow his conscience and speak against his own party slightly weakened his support from his fellow Republicans—but he would soon need all the support he could get.

six
Success and Scandal

When McCain entered the Senate in January 1987, he was an up and coming politician who had garnered national attention. He had only been in politics five years and it already looked as though he was destined for greater things. But by the end of the decade he would face a challenge that would nearly derail his career, and a great deal of his luster would be gone.

Although McCain had initially made his reputation dealing with foreign policy, he did not neglect domestic issues while in the House and the Senate. He made a commitment when he first came to the House to not neglect the Native Americans in Arizona. He had sponsored legislation to improve relations between the tribal governments and the federal government, extend federal leases for the tribes, and to relieve them of taxes and access fees. In addition to American Indian issues, he was also a sponsor of legislation to stiffen the penalties for child sex offenders.

After his 1986 election to the Senate, McCain was one of the top Republican vice presidential candidates in 1988. The Republican presidential field was crowded during the primaries, and the candidates all wanted McCain's endorsement.

One of the candidates was Senator Bob Dole of Kansas. McCain had grown close to Dole. Both men carried scars from combat. Dole had been severely wounded in the Italian campaign during World War II and had loss the use of an arm. McCain appreciated Dole for welcoming him warmly to the Senate and for assigning him to serve on important committees. But during the primaries McCain decided not to endorse any candidate, including then Vice President George H. W. Bush. He wanted the voters to decide who the Republican candidate would be, he said.

Vice President Bush eventually won the nomination. As the Republican National Convention neared, speculation that McCain would be Bush's running mate intensified. McCain made little public comment about the speculation. If disappointed when Bush selected Indiana senator Dan Quayle, he was careful to not show it in public. It was later revealed that Quayle had escaped serving in Vietnam by having an influential relative get him a highly sought appointment to the National Guard. When a reporter asked McCain if he had a problem with Quayle's selection after the draft controversy erupted, McCain said, "Well, only if he did get special favors to help him evade the draft." It had already been reported that Quayle had received "special favors," and the Bush campaign was furious at McCain for the comment.

McCain was asked to give a speech at the Republican National Convention. He was scheduled to speak the first night. His speech, entitled "Duty, Honor, Country," expressed

McCain's speech during the 1988 Republican National Convention garnered widespread admiration and support. This photo taken during the convention shows George H. W. Bush and his family on stage. *(Courtesy of AP Images)*

his patriotism. He recounted the heroics and determination of his fellow POWs during their captivity. He ended the speech by telling the audience about one POW who was repeatedly beaten for using bits of fabric to make American flags.

When McCain finished his speech he was given a standing ovation. The speech went out to a national audience and was publicized throughout the nation. It brought McCain a great deal of admiration and support.

George H. W. Bush began the election in 1988 far behind in the polls. But through a series of television commercials he managed to overcome his opponent, Massachusetts governor Michael Dukakis, and win handily in November. During the election, McCain traveled and campaigned for Bush and other Republicans running that year. However, although Bush won, the Republicans remained in the minority in both the House and Senate.

After his election, Bush began naming his cabinet selections. One of the most important cabinet jobs was secretary of defense—the manager of the vast bureaucracy that oversees all four branches of the military. The defense secretary is also responsible for approving new weapons systems, planes, and billions of dollars of other procurements.

McCain was pleased when Bush named former Republican Senator John Tower of Texas to be his secretary of defense. Tower had been McCain's favorite senator when he worked as the naval liaison. Tower was one of the most knowledgeable senators on national defense, the topic McCain cared about the most. He also enjoyed Tower's company and had traveled with him many times to other countries. Tower had also chaired the investigating committee that looked into the Iran-Contra Affair and his report had been respected

President George H. W. Bush appointed McCain's friend, Senator John Tower (below), to be his secretary of defense. *(Courtesy of the U.S. Department of Defense)*

for laying out the details without resorting to partisanship. McCain thought Tower both deserved the appointment and was by far the most qualified. But Tower's selection set off a controversy that deeply depressed, and infuriated, McCain.

Within days of Tower's selection, negative stories about him began appearing in newspapers. Most of the stories claimed Tower was a heavy drinker and that he had acted inappropriately toward women on his staff, as well as others.

The Senate has the responsibility of confirming the president's cabinet choices. If Tower was not approved first by the Senate Armed Services Committee, and then by the full Senate, he would not be able to serve as defense secretary. After the stories appeared, Tower's confirmation was in jeopardy.

McCain worked hard to get his old friend confirmed. He defended him during hearings in the Armed Services Committee, and worked behind the scenes to win other senators' support. But as support for Tower continued to slip, McCain began to lose his temper. At one point, when a senator opposed to Tower was speaking on the floor of the Senate, McCain sprung out of his seat and shouted the senator down. The Senate usually operates under a veil of decorum that conceals the intense feelings that often run beneath the surface. McCain's outburst was a violation of Senate custom and the first time his legendary temper was revealed to the nation at large.

In the end, McCain's work—and rage—were to no avail. When it became clear Tower would not be confirmed, President Bush withdrew his name from consideration and selected Dick Cheney, a representative from Wyoming, to be his secretary of defense.

McCain was deeply upset at how his old friend had been treated. He thought it was the lowest sort of politics, and within days, he would personally experience similar treatment.

McCain's involvement in what became known as the Keating Five scandal began quietly in 1987. Only weeks after he was sworn in as senator, McCain attended two meetings that almost ruined his political career.

The meetings were called so that McCain and a few other senators could meet with the chairman of the agency that oversaw the nation's savings and loans. Savings and loans were originally established to provide home mortgages. For decades, federal regulations limited the type of investments savings and loans could make, assuring that a high percentage of the loans were made in the relatively safe home mortgage market.

In the late 1970s and early 1980s, there was a drive to reduce or remove federal regulations throughout the economy. The idea was that regulations had grown too restrictive and were a drag on the economy. Most of the regulations that had limited savings and loans to mortgage loans were removed.

The removal of the rules on savings and loans were at the root of what became one of the worst financial disasters in U.S. history. Once they were free to make riskier and potentially more profitable investments, savings and loans became attractive takeover targets for real estate developers and others who were looking for a source of easy, cheap capital to finance their businesses. These investors began to buy controlling interest in savings and loans, offer higher returns on deposits in order to attract customers, and then use the deposits to invest in often risky projects. Some of the new owners of savings and loans also speculated in high-risk investments, such as unsecured bonds—called junk bonds—and other financial instruments much riskier than home mortgages. There were some dishonest new owners of savings and loans who simply plundered the deposits.

Charles Keating *(Courtesy of AP Images/Nick Ut)*

By the middle of the 1980s, a crisis was developing in the nation's savings and loans. Hundreds were about to go bankrupt. This created a major problem for the taxpayers, because most of the deposits in savings and loans were guaranteed by the federal government. When a savings and loans went bankrupt, or was closed by regulators working for the Federal Home Loan Bank Board, the agency responsible for monitoring the financial health of savings and loans, the taxpayers had to reimburse the deposits that had been lost. Making things worse was that many of the risky loans were made on speculative real estate projects that collapsed when the capital that was keeping them afloat dried up. This left the federal government holding billions of dollars worth of foreclosed real estate. Before it was over, the savings and loan debacle cost the taxpayers well over $500 billion.

The meetings McCain attended with officials of the Federal Home Loan Bank Board were on behalf of Charles Keating, a personal friend and one of his largest campaign contributors. McCain and his family had taken vacations with Keating and had flown on his personal jet. McCain had reimbursed Keating for the flights in some instances, but had failed to do so for other trips. Also, Cindy and her father had made investments in some of Keating's real estate developments, including a shopping center in Arizona. This personal and financial relationship with Keating would almost destroy McCain's Senate career.

The meeting was called at Keating's request. Keating owned one of the nation's largest savings and loans, Lincoln Financial. The Federal Home Loan Bank Board had recently issued new regulations that severely limited the amount of money savings and loans could invest in projects outside of home loans. It also began requiring that savings and loans keep more money in reserve to help carry them through downturns. This pushed Lincoln into trouble because of the bad loans it had made, most to Keating himself. Keating complained that the new rules would drive Lincoln into bankruptcy. He wanted McCain and a few other western senators he had befriended to intervene and ask the regulators to grant him a waiver from the new regulations.

After attending the two meetings, which he said were only fact-finding visits and were not attempts to pressure the bank examiners to grant special treatment, McCain told Keating there was nothing he could do. It was later revealed that Keating exploded at McCain for not pressuring the regulators. This was the last time McCain and Keating spoke. It was also later revealed that Keating had personally looted the savings and loan, transferring millions of dollars into his personal accounts as well as into his real estate developments. Lincoln was soon bankrupt; it was the largest of the hundreds of institutions to collapse. Keating was later indicted and convicted and was sentenced to five years in federal prison.

When it was revealed that McCain and the other senators had met with the regulators on Keating's behalf, he found himself in the middle of a scandal. It took months, but McCain was eventually cleared of any wrongdoing. Other senators, including McCain's colleague from Arizona, were not so lucky and were reprimanded by the Senate Ethics Committee for trying to pressure the board into granting Keating special treatment.

As the investigation dragged on it became a media sensation. The scandal surrounding the collapse of the savings

Three of the Keating Five, Sens. John Glenn (left), Dennis DeConccini (middle) and McCain, attend a Senate Ethics Committee hearing. *(Courtesy of AP Photo/John Duricka)*

and loan industry was a national outrage and the so-called Keating Five, McCain and four other senators, represented the entire debacle. Although it became clear that McCain had not gone over the line for his former friend, he was criticized for accepting contributions from Keating and for taking free trips on his personal plane.

The black mark on his reputation deeply troubled McCain. He considered himself to be an honest man who valued his integrity and character over success. It would take him years to recover from the ordeal, both personally and politically. That much of his involvement in the scandal was a result of taking campaign contributions from Keating would be one of the reasons he would later make campaign finance reform one of the central issues of his political career.

seven
New World

McCain continued to work as a senator throughout the Tower nomination fight and the Keating Five hearings. He was determined to not let the negative attention stop him from doing his work as senator.

By the late 1980s, the federal budget deficit—the difference between the amount of money that comes in each year and the amount of money spent—was larger than ever. It became a central political issue. McCain was a "budget hawk" who pushed for cuts in projects and programs and looked for ways to lower federal spending. He advocated giving the president the power to cut individual items out of spending bills, called the line item veto. He also pushed for congressional rules to stop representatives and senators from the funding of items specific to their states or districts—so-called pork barrel spending.

McCain remained involved in the ongoing conflict in Nicaragua and other parts of Central America. When it became clear that the dictator of Panama, Manuel Noriega, had no plans of allowing for democratic elections, and that he was deeply involved in the drug trade, McCain began to suggest a possible U.S. invasion of Panama to remove Noriega from power.

In December 1989, President Bush sent U.S. troops into Panama. Within days Noriega was captured and taken to a federal prison in Florida. He was later tried for drug trafficking and sentenced to a long prison term.

The world went through dramatic change during the first Bush administration. When Mikhail Gorbachev came to power in 1985, the Soviet Union was in trouble. The economy was in shambles and the military was bogged down in a war in Afghanistan. The people of the Soviet Union had been living under Communist control for almost seventy years and were growing tired of having their lives controlled by the huge bureaucracy.

Manuel Noriega is escorted onto a plane by agents from the U.S. Drug Enforcement Agency. *(Courtesy of the U.S. Department of Defense)*

Gorbachev set out to reform the economy and the political system. He and President Reagan met and signed a series of historic agreements to lower the number of nuclear weapons each country was pointing at the other.

Despite Gorbachev's best efforts, Soviet Communism was too unwieldy to be easily changed, and many members of the Communist government were opposed to reform. But Gorbachev's promise of reform had excited the people. First, the nations in Eastern Europe that had been under Soviet control since the end of World War II broke away and overthrew their Communist governments. In the Soviet Union there was a series of changes and events, beginning in 1990 and running through 1991, that ended Communist control. After a failed coup by diehard Communists in August 1991, the central government collapsed and the Soviet Union ceased to exist. The Cold War was over.

Much of John McCain's life had been defined by the Cold War. Both his and his father's military careers had focused on stopping the spread of communism. The Vietnam War had been justified to the American people as necessary to keep the remainder of Asia from becoming Communist. The end of the ideology that had taken so much from him was a great day for McCain. But he realized that there were many other conflicts and near conflicts in the world that would now need U.S. attention.

In August 1990, Saddam Hussein, the dictator of Iraq, sent troops into oil-rich Kuwait, the country's southern neighbor. For most of the 1980s, Iraq had been locked into a horrific war with its eastern neighbor Iran. At the war's end Iraq was in economic chaos and Saddam wanted the oil in Kuwait to help alleviate his financial problems. Hussein annexed

McCain supported President George H. W. Bush's resolution authorizing military action to drive Iraqi troops out of Kuwait. In this 1991 photo, a U.S. battleship shells Iraqi targets along the northern Kuwaiti coast. *(Courtesy of the U.S. Department of Defense)*

Kuwait on August 9, and his soldiers began rounding up and sometimes killing anyone they suspected of opposing Iraqi control.

Although President Bush had initially promised Hussein the U.S. would not invade to protect Kuwait, he changed his mind under international pressure. After weeks of futile negotiations the United Nations passed a resolution authorizing military action to drive Iraqi troops out of Kuwait. Hussein refused to retreat.

On January 16, 1991, the U.S. and its allies launched air strikes and missile attacks against Iraqi troops in Kuwait and on the Iraqi capital of Baghdad. These attacks continued for more than a month. A massive invasion of more than 400,000 ground troops began on February 23; on February 26, Saddam pulled his troops out of Kuwait.

The Gulf War occurred during McCain's Keating Five travails, but he still threw himself into supporting President Bush's invasion plans. Some senators wanted to impose strict sanctions on Iraq, limiting food, drugs, and other supplies into the country until Saddam pulled out of Kuwait. They saw it as a better alternative to invasion. McCain argued strenuously against sanctions because innocent people would suffer and they would have little impact on Saddam's military decisions:

> Who are the ones who would suffer as a result of sanctions? In my view, it is the innocent civilians, children, and others that Saddam Hussein would view as nonessentials in his war efforts. If we drag out this crisis and we don't at some time bring it to a successful resolution, we face a prospect of another Vietnam War.

Once he was finally cleared of wrongdoing in the Keating affair, McCain worked hard at restoring his reputation and preparing for his reelection campaign in 1992. He wrote editorials for Arizona newspapers explaining why he advocated military action against Saddam Hussein. He helped to defeat a health insurance reform bill that he said would unfairly affect senior citizens—Arizona is one of the nation's most popular retirement states. He also continued his work to cut federal spending, and supported an amendment to the U.S. Constitution requiring a balanced budget and helped to forge an agreement in Congress that was supposed to reduce the deficit in five years.

Although his political future had seemed at risk only a few months before, McCain faced only token opposition in his 1992 reelection bid. Early on he was again concerned that

Bruce Babbitt, who had lost his 1988 bid for the Democratic presidential nomination, would oppose him. Once Babbitt announced he was not running there was little chance McCain would be defeated. The 1992 victory went a long way toward redeeming his reputation after the fallout from the Keating affair.

Although McCain easily won reelection in 1992, President Bush did not fare so well. As late as spring of 1991, after the quick victory in Iraq, Bush had the highest poll ratings ever recorded. But the economy began to slip into a recession and the president, who had always been more focused on foreign affairs, began to slip. Many people wondered if he was as focused as he should have been on their problems. When Democratic nominee Bill Clinton, governor of Arkansas, surprised the Bush campaign with an aggressive, well-run campaign, the president was not able to recover. That fall, as McCain was celebrating his victory, President Bush lost to Clinton in a three-way race.

McCain was sad to see Bush defeated. He thought he had provided strong leadership when it was needed and deserved a second term. Regardless, he returned to Washington determined to work with the new president.

Even before the election, McCain had begun working closely with a Democratic senator to try to solve one of the last issues left from the Vietnam War. Only weeks after the Gulf War ended, McCain had taken another trip to Vietnam. He traveled with Senator John Kerry of Massachusetts, who had also served and been wounded in Vietnam. The goal of the trip was to hopefully finally determine if there were any more American prisoners being held in Vietnam. The issue of the MIAs was at a near fever pitch. Soon after McCain

Senator Kerry and McCain attend a hearing of the Senate Select Committee on POW/MIA Affairs. *(Courtesy of AP Images/John Duricka)*

returned from Vietnam, *Newsweek* magazine ran a cover story with a picture that MIA groups said was of three American men still being held in Vietnam. The photo was later proved to be a forgery, but the passions of the MIA families were running high. They assumed McCain would come back from Vietnam with evidence there were still MIAs alive.

When Kerry returned from Vietnam in the early 1970s, he had become one of the leading protesters against the war. He had formed a group called Vietnam Veterans Against the War and testified before Congress about the group and why they advocated an immediate U.S. withdrawal. Many veterans thought Kerry had betrayed them by his testimony, and the controversy continued to follow him. (His antiwar activities would become a major issue when Kerry ran for president in 2004.)

McCain had been wary of Kerry when he first came to the Senate. However, they had finally had a long conversation and made peace, becoming close enough to work on the MIA issue together. They hoped a bipartisan effort would help to end the issue.

When they returned from Vietnam, McCain was careful to not make many public statements. The group he and Kerry headed would release a report that would explain what they had found on their trip and their recommendations for the future.

McCain, Kerry, and the other members of the Senate Select Committee on POW/MIA Affairs hoped their report would end the controversy and help to settle the painful questions and doubts of the families.

The report was not issued until 1993, only days before Clinton took office as president. Clinton had worked to avoid being drafted during the war, which had angered many Americans, particularly Vietnam veterans, when it was revealed. The Clinton revelations had put the Vietnam War back into the news.

McCain and Kerry's report was based on months of investigations, trips to Vietnam, and questioning of former government officials. Its conclusion was that "while some information remains yet to be investigated, there is, at this time, no compelling evidence that proves any American remains alive in captivity in Southeast Asia."

It was soon obvious that the 1,223-page report was not going to quiet the most insistent of the MIA groups. Instead, they were angered by what they saw as McCain's desertion of the issue. While some of the families and groups accepted the report, others saw it as part of a government conspiracy

McCain and Cindy pose with their children: (from left to right) Meghan, Bridget, James, and John Sidney IV. *(Courtesy of AP Images)*

designed to hide the fact that the U.S. government had left people behind in its haste to leave Vietnam. McCain made many public comments about the report and the evidence it included. However, he had now antagonized a vocal group of his former supporters who would oppose him vociferously when he ran for president in 2000.

As McCain had pursued his political career, his family had continued to grow. After the birth of his first child with Cindy, Meghan, they had two sons, John Sidney IV and James. He and Cindy also adopted a girl they named Bridget from an orphanage in Bangladesh.

McCain's family was a source of joy and support for him, but he and Cindy did face one challenge. Cindy revealed in 1994 that she had developed an addiction to pain killers following back surgery. She had convinced doctors to write her prescriptions. She had also used a charity she ran that provided medical service to people who could not afford to acquire prescriptions for drugs. After her family confronted her about her problem she managed to kick her dependency and went public with her problem. She also admitted using her charitable organization to get drugs. She was investigated but not indicted after she agreed to enter treatment.

eight
Maverick

After the election of Bill Clinton to the presidency in 1992, the Republicans were out of power. Both houses of Congress and the presidency were in control of Democrats. Partisan fighting between the Democrats and the remaining congressional Republicans began almost immediately.

During this period, and throughout the eight years of the Clinton administration, McCain began to separate himself from his more partisan colleagues. He opposed many of Clinton's initiatives, and sternly criticized his management of foreign affairs—and even voted to remove him from office in 1999—but he avoided many of the bitter political fights that characterized the decade.

One of the first controversial issues in 1993 was Clinton's attempt to remove the restriction against open homosexuals and lesbians serving in the military. The vast majority of Republicans were opposed to the change. They were also

Although McCain opposed many of President Clinton's initiatives, he began to separate himself from highly partisan members of his party during Clinton's administration. *(Courtesy of AP Images/Marcy Nighswander)*

opposed to a proposed compromise called "Don't Ask, Don't Tell," which was supposed to allow homosexuals and lesbians to serve if they remained silent about their sexuality. McCain supported the compromise.

McCain's most controversial stance, as regards his relationship with other Republicans, during Clinton's first term was his endorsement of diplomatic recognition of Vietnam. Earlier, the commission he had chaired with John Kerry reported there was no compelling evidence that POWs remained in Vietnam. Then, soon after Clinton took office, McCain announced he was encouraging the president to recognize the country he had been held prisoner in for over six years. This, combined with the MIA/POW report, angered a large number of veterans and families of missing servicemen—as well as many politicians on the right.

McCain ended up opposing Clinton most often on foreign and military policy. He argued against sending more troops into the African nation of Somalia. The troops were supposed to be peacekeepers between warring groups. Tragically, they were attacked; two dead soldiers were dragged through the streets of Mogadishu, the capital city. Soon after, Clinton ordered the removal of all U.S. troops.

McCain also opposed Clinton when he sent troops into Haiti to restore the democratically elected president, Jean-Bertrand Aristide, to power. McCain argued that it would be years before order was restored in the chaotic country and that the mission was not worth the risk.

McCain also had strong feelings about the situation in Iraq. He thought President Bush had made a mistake by not removing Saddam Hussein from power following the Gulf War, and that Clinton was letting another serious problem develop.

In general, McCain's frustration with what he saw as Clinton's unwillingness to use the power of the U.S. military to address foreign policy problems led him to become, in his own words, "a constant and often caustic critic of the many conceptual and operational failures of Clinton's foreign and defense policies." He was frustrated at Clinton's inclination to "use the least force possible" when faced with a crisis.

McCain insisted he always made his decisions on what he thought was best for the country before he thought of the political ramifications of his decisions. This led him to sometimes support Clinton when most of his colleagues did not. When Clinton wanted the Senate to vote in support of his plan to send 20,000 U.S. troops to help keep the peace in the war-torn Balkans, McCain worked to convince reluctant Republicans to vote in favor of the resolution. Most Republicans argued that the U.S. did not have an interest in helping to end the atrocities and ethnic murder suffered by the Bosnian Muslims and other minorities in the Balkans. McCain argued that the president had committed U.S. troops and it was the responsibility of the Senate to support the troops when they were in harm's way. His stance was not popular, but the resolution passed.

The other Republican who argued to support President Clinton in sending troops to the Balkans was Senate Majority Leader Bob Dole. During the 1996 race for the Republican presidential nomination, Dole was challenged by McCain's friend, Senator Phil Gramm of Texas. McCain was committed to supporting Gramm but was not unhappy when Dole won. At the Republican Convention that summer McCain was again mentioned as a possible vice presidential candidate, but in the end Dole did not select him. Dole went on to lose to President Clinton in the fall.

In addition to his work in promoting his foreign policy ideas, McCain continued his efforts to stop what he considered to be wasteful spending. However, he became most identified with two characteristically controversial domestic issues.

Ever since the connection between smoking and cancer had been established in the 1960s there had been a series of government attempts to cut down on the use of tobacco. The tobacco companies were opposed to the efforts and used its vast resources to stop the changes. Restricting the sale and

McCain attends an anti-tobacco rally on Capitol Hill in this 1998 photo. *(Courtesy of AP Images/Dennis Cook)*

advertising of cigarettes and tobacco products, especially to the young, had been a long, difficult slog for over thirty years.

When McCain was appointed chairman of the Senate's commerce committee in 1996, he began working on anti-smoking legislation. In true McCain fashion, he made one of his first announcements of his plans in Florence, South Carolina, in the heart of tobacco country. "More than 3000 children start smoking everyday in this country," he said. He went on to say that although his plan would compensate tobacco farmers, its primary goal was to drastically reduce the number of children who took up smoking.

McCain cooperated with the Clinton administration to push the antismoking bill in Congress. Again, he was opposed by most senators from his party. This time, assisted by the multimillion dollar ad campaign paid for by the tobacco industry,

McCain's legislation was killed by a filibuster. In a filibuster, opponents take the floor and refuse to yield until the legislation is pulled from consideration. A vote to end a filibuster, called cloture, requires sixty votes to succeed.

McCain also antagonized his party, as well as many Democrats, when he joined forces with Senator Russ Feingold of Wisconsin, a Democrat, to propose a bill to reform how political campaigns are financed. The main feature of the McCain-Feingold bill would limit what was called "soft money," which are funds given to the political parties and groups supporting a candidate instead of to the candidate directly. Soft money contributions avoided the existing limits on the amount an individual could contribute to a campaign.

McCain-Feingold was highly unpopular in both parties initially. McCain was accused of trying to limit free speech and was even called antidemocratic. Despite the often vociferous attacks on him from both sides, McCain stubbornly stuck to the bill—even after it suffered defeat after defeat. It would take years before he would see it enacted.

Russ Feingold and McCain smile during a rally following a vote on campaign finance reform. *(Courtesy of AP Images/Dennis Cook)*

In 1999, McCain voted to remove President Clinton from office. Clinton was charged with lying about his sexual relationship with a White House intern.

McCain insisted his vote was based on principle, not politics, but he was certainly thinking about politics in 1999. After easily being reelected to the Senate in 1998, he began to set his sights on the presidency. He knew he would not be the favorite to win the Republican nomination. He had antagonized many in his party with his independent approach to politics. He also knew that Governor George W. Bush of Texas, son of the former president, had already signed up the largest donors and many of the best consultants.

McCain acknowledged he wanted to be president, but he also thought his type of approach to the critical issues and problems was what the country needed. On April 14, 1999, he announced he would be a candidate for president in 2000.

nine
Straight Talk

Speculation that McCain would run for president in 2000 had begun days after Bob Dole lost to President Bill Clinton in 1996. Many of those who thought McCain would run, and even several who were actively encouraging him to run, thought he had only a slim chance of winning the Republican nomination.

McCain's reputation for honesty had been hurt by the Keating affair. He had worked hard to repair the damage, and none of the official reports charged him with wrongdoing, but the intense media coverage had done damage.

McCain's biggest obstacle, however, was within the Republican Party. The party leaders had been deeply bitter ever since Bill Clinton had defeated George H. W. Bush in 1992. It was a stunning defeat, and after the Republicans won control of both the House and the Senate in the 1994 midterm elections, most party leaders thought Clinton would be defeated easily in 1996. But Dole had been unable to unseat the president, and the major contributors to the party and the influential leaders were determined to align behind one candidate in 2000 and to make sure he won the nomination and the general election. It was obvious that they did not want McCain to be that candidate.

The activist conservative groups, including those on the so-called Religious Right, which had become powerful in the Republican Party, were aligned behind George W. Bush. They were incensed about McCain's attempts to reform how campaigns were funded, and they argued that the McCain-Feingold bill would seriously cripple their ability to raise money and elect candidates that supported their beliefs. Bush made it known that he was opposed to McCain-Feingold and that he agreed with the Religious Right on all their political positions.

McCain refused to alter his support of campaign finance reform. When he began traveling the country and making speeches in preparation to run for president, he made it clear that it would be the centerpiece of his campaign. Another principal issue—and another that did not endear him to many in his party—was his insistence on paying off the federal debt before passing huge

During his 2000 campaign for president, McCain didn't campaign in Iowa so he could focus on winning the New Hampshire primary. In this photo, McCain wears a New Hampshire baseball cap during his campaign in that state. *(Courtesy of AP Images/Jim Cole)*

tax cuts. McCain advocated a more moderate tax cut than the one proposed by Bush. McCain also promised to make improvements on the so-called entitlement programs, such as Medicare and Social Security.

After he decided to run for president, McCain made one major strategic decision that he knew was a gamble. Most candidates in both parties began the primary campaign trying to win the Iowa caucuses, which traditionally are held a few days before the first primary in New Hampshire. McCain announced he would skip Iowa, where Bush already had an advantage, and concentrate on winning New Hampshire.

From the beginning, McCain was behind Bush in the polls. He also lagged far behind in fund-raising—which was made worse by his refusal to accept soft money. Bush had the support of the vast majority of the wealthy contributors. He also had the name recognition that came from being the son of the former president. The last thing party heavyweights wanted was a serious challenge from the maverick senator from Arizona.

McCain and his advisers decided to make the most of his renegade reputation. When McCain officially announced he was running, in Nashua, New Hampshire, on September 27, 1999, he stated that his first goal was to rid politics of the corruption caused by the vast amount of money politicians had to raise to compete. In effect, he was telling the leaders of his own party he had no intention of altering his message to curry their favor. He also promised to both reform and strengthen the U.S. military, and to run a strong, confident foreign policy. He concluded by saying "It is because I owe America more than she has ever owed me that I am a candidate for president."

To further drive home the point that he was a different type of candidate, McCain labeled his campaign bus the Straight Talk Express. He also allowed an unprecedented number of reporters to travel with him. He was usually available to answer their questions and actually seemed to enjoy the give and take of their conversations.

This was a risky move. Politicians are always susceptible to making misstatements or being misunderstood. Most avoid situations where they could make a verbal gaffe, sticking to highly scripted speeches and events. But McCain knew he needed to try a different approach.

The Straight Talk Express worked better than McCain or his advisor could have imagined. Most reporters appreciated not being so tightly controlled and responded to the access, and McCain's candor, positively. Soon the Bush campaign

McCain and his wife, Cindy, stand in front of the "Straight Talk Express" bus during a 2000 press conference. *(Courtesy of AP Images/ Charlie Neibergall)*

was grumbling about what they called the preferential treatment McCain received.

The Straight Talk Express was not the only gamble that paid off. McCain's decision to skip Iowa and focus on New Hampshire also turned out to be a smart move. Bush began with a strong lead, but as McCain traveled the state, holding dozens of town meetings in which individual citizens could ask questions, and giving interviews to local television stations and newspapers, he began to gain on Bush.

As McCain turned into a serious threat, rumors began to circulate. The Bush campaign denied starting the rumors, but it was pointed out repeatedly by reporters that the rumors didn't start until Bush began losing ground.

Perhaps the most outlandish—and hurtful—rumor was that McCain had been so severely damaged psychologically in Vietnam that he was not suitable to be president. McCain had long admitted to having a quick temper but that had existed before his years as a POW. To combat the whispering campaign, McCain released his medical records. The records revealed that he had been analyzed when he was released and found to be of sound mind. Ironically, the psychologists who interviewed him found that his Vietnam experiences had probably improved his mental health by forcing him to be more accepting of others and patient in the face of disappointment or stress. He now had a bigger perspective on life and was not as prone to take relatively minor problems as seriously as he had before.

McCain was initially determined to push past the negative attacks to continue to win votes by pushing his reform agenda. He promised to restore integrity to the presidency.

The Bush campaign had been slow to respond to the Straight

Talk Express as it traveled the state garnering good reviews. It was almost a fatal mistake. The New Hampshire primary was held on February 1, 2000. At the end of the night John McCain had pulled off an upset, winning over Bush by a margin of 49 percent to Bush's 31 percent. (The remainder of the votes were split among other candidates.)

The Bush campaign was stunned, and angry. How angry they were would soon become clear.

The next major primary was in South Carolina. It was going to be a showdown. Although both candidates promised to continue after South Carolina, the loser would face an almost insurmountable challenge. Both sides were determined to win what several observers would come to call the dirtiest campaign in American political history.

McCain addresses a crowd during his 2000 presidential campaign. *(Courtesy of AP Images/Steven Senne)*

After his win in New Hampshire, McCain was several points ahead in the polls in South Carolina. He left for South Carolina right after his victory speech the night of the New Hampshire primary. When he landed, thousands of enthusiastic supporters greeted him when he stepped off the plane.

Also waiting for him were negative television commercials paid for by the Bush campaign and other groups that supported Bush. Although Bush and McCain had made an agreement, sealed by a handshake, to not engage in negative attacks on each other, the loss in New Hampshire had raised the stakes, and the Bush camp reneged on their word.

More hurtful and damaging rumors were spread about McCain. Bush even appeared on stage with a man who accused McCain of being a traitor to his country while in Vietnam and of selling out his fellow POWs during their captivity. The old stories that he was psychologically damaged started again, despite the fact he had earlier released his medical records.

Not satisfied to question his integrity, patriotism, and sanity, other rumors accused McCain of giving his wife a venereal disease, having an affair with an actress, and fathering a child out of wedlock.

McCain struggled to fight against the bitter attacks. He was hampered, however, because Bush's campaign had an overwhelming financial advantage. McCain ran commercials defending his political positions but was powerless against the more base charges.

By the end of the South Carolina primary, McCain was exhausted, angry, and dispirited. Although he had expected a tough campaign, he later admitted he might have been naïve to not realize the depths the leaders of his party would go to in order to deny him the nomination.

Bush won the South Carolina primary by a margin of 10 percent. After his loss, McCain called Bush to congratulate him, but those close to him knew he was deeply angry.

McCain vowed to continue his campaign. The new major primary state was Michigan, where the race was again ugly. He won the Michigan primary, as well as the one in Arizona the same day.

George W. Bush listens as McCain speaks during a Republican presidential debate. *(Courtesy of AP Images/Gary Fandel)*

McCain knew the final showdown between him and Bush would come on Super Tuesday, a day when there would be Republican primaries in twelve states. Because Bush had a lead in delegates, McCain would have to sweep all the primaries, or at least ten of them, to remain a serious challenger. Among the states holding primaries were California, New York, Massachusetts, and Virginia.

McCain was still angry about the South Carolina primary. He knew some of the worst attacks had come from the so-called Religious Right, a powerful block in the Republican Party. McCain had come to think the Religious Right had too much power in his party. He was also incensed at how they had attacked him and his family.

Virginia was home to several of the most powerful of the religious groups. Characteristically, McCain decided to make his opinions about the Religious Right clear in a speech he delivered at a high school in Virginia Beach, Virginia, the hometown of Pat Robertson, the founder of the Christian Coalition and a pioneer at using cable television to advance his agenda and to raise money.

McCain lashed out at what he called "a few self-appointed leaders" who were using the Republican Party to advance their own political power. Those leaders, he said, "distort my pro-life positions and smear the reputations of my supporters" because he did not "ascribe to their failed philosophy that money is our message." In short, they unjustly attacked him not because they disagreed with him on fundamental issues, but because he wanted to limit the amount of money that could be used in politics.

The speech captured an enormous amount of media attention. Super Tuesday was the next day, however, and it was soon clear that although many in his party considered the speech to be brave, it did little to earn him votes. Bush won the majority of the states on Super Tuesday, winning Virginia by a margin of 53 percent to 44 percent.

There were a few other primaries ahead, but the race was over. Bush had too much money and too much support from the powerful people in the Republican Party. McCain had run a valiant and unusually open campaign that earned him the votes of millions and the respect of millions more, but he would not be president in 2000. That summer at the Republican Convention in Philadelphia, George W. Bush became the Republican nominee for president.

ten

Another Try

McCain spoke at the Republican Convention in 2000. He made it clear that he was a loyal member of the party, regardless of how he felt about the primary campaign, and would support George Bush in the general election. "I support him," he said about Bush. "I am grateful to him. I am proud of him. He is a good man from a good family that has, in good times and bad, dedicated themselves to America."

McCain spoke on Tuesday night. The next day he was at Bethesda Naval Hospital in Washington. During a physical, doctors performed a biopsy on some spots from his head and arm. A few days later he found out that he had melanoma, the most serious type of skin cancer because it can spread rapidly into other organs.

McCain went to the Mayo Clinic for more tests that confirmed the earlier diagnosis. The next day he was in surgery for more than five hours. When he recovered from the surgery, the doctors told him they thought they had got all the cancer and that it had not spread. He was released two days later and went home to Arizona to recuperate for several days.

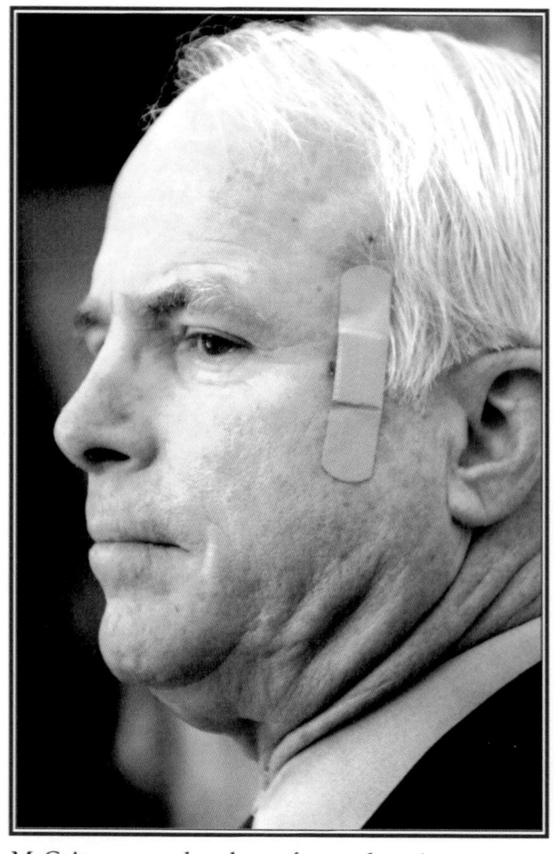

McCain wears a bandage after undergoing surgery to remove a section of cancerous skin. *(Courtesy of AP Images/Eric Draper)*

After spending a short time recuperating, McCain hit the campaign trail for Bush. Those closest to him could tell he still had resentment toward Bush and his campaign, but he was careful to keep it out of the press and to not let the public see it. McCain was clearly convinced that a Republican victory was the best thing for the country and did all he could do to make sure it would happen.

The 2000 presidential election turned out to be the closest and most hotly contested in modern U.S. history. Because of the near tie in Florida and irregularities in how the ballots were tabulated, the election was in dispute for days. It was not until December 12, 2000, when the U.S. Supreme

Court, in a 5-4 decision on party lines, decided that Bush would be the next president.

Coming to the presidency by a decision of the Supreme Court meant Bush did not initially have an overwhelming mandate. He had lost the popular vote and millions of Americans were angry at the court's decision.

McCain had made campaign finance reform the centerpiece of his presidential campaign. The American people, he insisted, should have a clean, honest political system. At stop after stop he returned to this central message, even when he knew he was before an audience that did not support it. Although it became evident his insistence on campaign reform was not popular to many Republican primary voters, he refused to stop speaking about it.

After the Supreme Court upheld election results that made Bush president, McCain intensified his effort to get campaign finance reform through Congress. Because Bush, who was vocally opposed to the McCain-Feingold legislation, was coming into office without a large mandate, McCain thought it provided a strong opportunity to pass the legislation. Although the bill was not popular with the president, or in Washington, it was very popular nationwide. He hoped Bush would not risk antagonizing the voters by vetoing the bill—if he could get it through the House and the Senate.

Although McCain thought the political dynamic was shaping up in his favor, he knew there was much work to be done. Even while recuperating from cancer surgery, he lobbied his colleagues. Earlier attempts to pass campaign finance reform had been filibustered. The last attempt to end the filibuster of campaign finance reform was one vote short.

One of the Republicans who had voted against cloture previously told McCain that this time he would provide the needed last vote. Campaign finance reform, the issue closest to McCain's heart, would finally make it to a floor vote, where it could be voted up and down by the entire Senate.

McCain held a press conference to announce he had enough votes to end a filibuster and that he was going to reintroduce the legislation even before Bush was inaugurated. Everyone assembled knew he was throwing down the gauntlet—letting the new president know he was going to challenge him on this issue, just as he had during the campaign.

The McCain-Feingold bill would end "soft money" contributions to campaigns, limit some advertising by outside groups, and require union leaders to get permission from their members before donating union dues to campaigns or political parties. In another press conference after reintroducing the bill, McCain said that Americans "want their government back," and McCain-Feingold would give it to them.

After he was sworn in, President Bush tried to pressure McCain to wait to introduce his bill. He even invited him to the White House for a meeting, one-on-one. McCain refused to wait. It was clear there was still tension between them. The fight between McCain and Bush became one of the most discussed feuds in Washington. The relationship was so bad there were even rumors circulating that McCain was considering leaving the Republican Party to become a Democrat.

The political spat involved other issues. McCain criticized the president for not taking environmental problems, including global warming, more seriously. He voted against Bush's centerpiece of his economic plan, a large tax cut, because he said it was fiscally irresponsible and benefited the wealthy at the expense of the middle class. At home in Arizona, a group of conservative Republican supporters of President Bush even started a recall campaign in hopes of forcing McCain out of the Senate.

The political dynamic in Washington and the nation at large changed suddenly on September 11, 2001. That day Islamic terrorists seized four airliners loaded with passengers. Two of the planes were flown into the two towers of the World Trade Center in lower Manhattan. Another was flown into the Pentagon, the headquarters of the U.S. military outside of Washington; the other crashed in Pennsylvania on its way back to Washington. Nearly 3,000 innocent people were killed.

The attacks stunned the nation and the world. They also brought Bush and McCain together. A few days after the attacks, McCain said, "This is as serious a threat as we, in our nation, have ever faced." He said he was going to work with the president and others to make sure it never happened again.

One of McCain's first actions was to cosponsor legislation to create a commission to investigate exactly what happened on September 11 and to determine what went wrong.

Although he was committed to tracking down the terrorists, and trying to prevent future attacks, McCain did not take his focus off of campaign finance reform, as it was too important of an issue. This time he was successful in getting both the House and Senate to pass the campaign finance bill.

The next question was whether or not President Bush would sign the bill into law, or would he veto it. After waiting days, Bush announced he would sign McCain-Feingold—but hoped it would be overturned in the federal courts. There is usually a ceremony when a bill in signed. The sponsoring senators and representatives are invited to the White House, and there is press coverage. Bush signed McCain-Feingold early in the morning, alone, without media. He wanted his signing to have as little attention as possible.

Less than a month after the September 11 attacks, President Bush ordered an invasion of Afghanistan, which was under the control of the Taliban, an extremist Islamic group. The Taliban had provided a home and protection for al-Qaeda, the group that carried out the attacks. Its leader, Osama bin Laden, had lived in Afghanistan since the Taliban had taken over.

U.S. forces, fighting with local Afghani leaders, were able to drive the Taliban from power by the end of November. However, Osama bin Laden and most of the Taliban leadership escaped to the wild, mountainous border of Afghanistan and Pakistan. McCain spoke out in support of overthrowing the Taliban, but regretted the escape of bin Laden.

As the Afghan invasion was taking place, members of the Bush administration began planning an invasion of Iraq. Their goal was to overthrow Saddam Hussein.

Since his defeat in 1991, Saddam had continued to brutalize his people and to resist adhering to the terms he had accepted after his defeat. One of the principal terms of the agreement was to stop building nuclear and chemical weapons. Saddam was supposed to allow weapons inspectors, working under the auspices of the United Nations, to freely travel in Iraq and to inspect all potential weapon factories when and however they wanted. Saddam consistently resisted the inspections and in 1998 he threw the inspectors out of Iraq.

Officials in the Bush administration insisted Saddam had developed dangerous weapons since 1998 and had hidden them. These weapons, they said, could be given to the terrorists. They also argued that overthrowing Saddam and replacing him with a democratic government would help to stop the growing terrorist threat and put the volatile region on the path to democracy. Finally, they linked Saddam to the September 11 attacks, though they did not specify how.

Invading Iraq was a controversial issue throughout 2002 and into 2003. Opponents of the invasion saw it as foolish to invade with so little evidence that Saddam had dangerous weapons and doubted it would be possible to create a democratic Iraq. Proponents said there were probably weapons in Iraq and that Saddam was a dangerous man who hated the U.S. and would stop at nothing to destroy

McCain and other Congressmen watch as President Bush signs a resolution authorizing the use of force against Iraq. *(Courtesy of AP Images/Ron Edmonds)*

it. The logical next step in the war on terror, they said, was to remove him from power.

As Bush and other members of his administration advocated for the war, McCain joined them. He was an early supporter of the invasion. He and Bush began to move closer as they publicly and actively supported the invasion of Iraq.

McCain spoke in support of a Senate resolution supporting the invasion of Iraq on October 2, 2002. "America is at war with terrorists who murdered our people one year ago," he said, linking Saddam to the attacks on September 11—although there was no evidence of the linkage. He went on to argue that the Senate should not tie the hands of the president, and should let him pursue the dangers facing the country as he thought best. The resolution passed.

McCain speaks with Lt. Gen. Ray Odierno at Camp Ramadi, Iraq. Although McCain has openly criticized the Bush administration's management of the war, he remains committed to keeping troops in Iraq. *(Courtesy of the U.S. Department of Defense)*

The U.S., supported by Great Britain, Australia, and a few other countries, launched the attack on Iraq on March 23, 2003. After fierce fighting, Baghdad, the capital city, fell and Saddam fled. He was later captured and was executed in 2006.

Initially, most of the Iraqi people were happy to be rid of Saddam and were grateful to the U.S. But by that summer, public opinion in Iraq had changed and a series of bombings and other attacks against U.S. forces began. In addition, there had long been tension and violence between members of the two major branches of Islam, Shia and Sunni, as well as conflict between the Arab population and the ethnic Kurdish minority. Without the brutal hand of Saddam, the age-old conflicts erupted into sectarian violence.

As the 2004 elections approached, the deteriorating situation in Iraq had begun to make the war unpopular in the U.S. There were even fears among Republicans that Bush was vulnerable because of mismanagement of the war.

The Democrats nominated McCain's old friend John Kerry to run against Bush. It was rumored that Kerry wanted McCain to be his running mate. McCain denied the rumors and campaigned actively for Bush's reelection. If he still retained anger from the 2000 race, he hid it as he traveled with Bush on the campaign trail. Bush was reelected in November.

As the political and military situation in Iraq continued to worsen after the election, McCain began to openly criticize the president for his management of the war. He singled out Defense Secretary Donald Rumsfeld for biting criticism. At one point, he said that Rumsfeld was the worst defense secretary in history. He still supported the war, however, and argued that it was simply too important to quit before the

U.S. had won. If the U.S. left too soon, he said, the country would become a haven for terrorists and the U.S. would lose all credibility in the region. Even as the sectarian conflict grew bloodier—and the causality numbers increased—McCain insisted the U.S. not leave. "I believe the consequences of failure are catastrophic," he said in 2006.

McCain was locked into supporting what he called a botched policy and a president he was not close to, because he believed staying in Iraq was the right thing to do.

By the 2006 midterm elections, the war had few supporters remaining. The Republicans suffered stinging defeats all over the country. They lost control of both houses of Congress.

McCain officially announces his candidacy for the 2008 presidential election. *(Photo courtesy of River Bissonnette)*

Immediately after the 2006 elections, speculation intensified that McCain would run for president in 2008. If he was elected, however, McCain would be seventy-two when he took office. In addition, he had a history of cancer. He was also, despite his support of Bush, still not popular in his party.

Despite the odds against him, McCain announced that he would be a candidate for the presidency in 2008. In many ways he faced a tougher challenge than in 2000. That earlier campaign had antagonized many in his own party, and even with his steadfast support of the unpopular war, McCain had an uphill battle to get his party's nomination.

McCain had never hesitated from taking on a challenge. His last campaign for the presidency might turn out to be his biggest challenge of all.

Timeline

1935 John Sidney McCain III born on August 29.

1958 Graduates from the Naval Academy in Annapolis, Virginia; attends naval flight training school in Florida.

1965 Marries Carol Shepp.

1967 Assigned to aircraft carrier patrolling North Vietnam; crashes plane over Hanoi, captured by Vietcong and imprisoned at "Hanoi Hilton" POW camp.

1973 Released from POW camp after six years of imprisonment and torture.

1976 Becomes naval liaison to U.S. Senate, befriends numerous senators and politicians.

1980 Divorces Carol Shepp; marries Cindy Hensley.

1981 Retires from Navy; moves to Arizona with Hensley, goes to work for her father's company.

1982 Elected to U.S. House of Representatives, representing Arizona's First District.

1985 Returns to Vietnam as part of television special with journalist Walter Cronkite.

1986 Elected to U.S. Senate.

1987 Supports Reagan administration in the Iran-Contra scandal, antagonizing other Republican politicians; involved in the Keating Five scandal.

1988 Speaks at Republican National Convention; campaigns for the presidency of George H. W. Bush.

1991 Supports Gulf War.

1996 As chairman of Senate Commerce Committee, pushes for anti-smoking legislation and begins pushing McCain-Weingold campaign finance bill; both actions antagonize fellow Republicans.

2000 Runs for president of U.S., but is largely not backed by Republican party; attracts media and popular support with Straight Talk Express, beating frontrunner George W. Bush in several primary elections; concedes the election to Bush, bowing to increased pressure and attacks from Republicans and the Religious Right; speaks at Republican National Convention, giving his support to Bush; found to have melanoma, but it is treated.

2001 Continues pushing McCain-Weingold campaign finance bill, against the opposition of President Bush; gets the bill passed by the end of the year; opposes Bush on economic and some environmental issues; after terrorist attacks on September 11, helps sponsor legislation creating the 9/11 Commission to investigate the attacks; supports Bush's plan to invade Afghanistan.

2003 Supports Bush's plan to invade Iraq.

2004 Supports Bush's reelection campaign against John Kerry; criticizes Bush's secretary of defense, Donald Rumsfeld, but continues to support Iraq war.

2007 Announces his run for president in 2008 on the *Late Show With David Letterman*.

Sources

CHAPTER ONE: First Son

p. 9, "He knew his number . . ." Robert Timberg, *John McCain: An American Odyssey* (New York: Simon & Schuster, 1999) 19.

p. 13, "I have never forgotten . . ." John McCain and Mark Salter, *Faith of My Fathers: A Family Memoir* (New York: Random House, 1999) 116.

p. 15, "Captain, please don't do . . ." Ibid., 131.

p. 15, "gross disorder," Ibid., 142.

CHAPTER THREE: POW

p. 26, "You don't have to . . ." Timberg, *John McCain: An American Odyssey*, 77.

p. 29, "Take me to the . . ." McCain and Salter, *Faith of My Fathers*, 191.

p. 31, "I wanted to say . . ." Ibid., 235.

CHAPTER FOUR: From Hanoi to Congress

p. 35, "Well, you know, I . . ." Timberg, *John McCain: An American* Odyssey, 111.

p. 45, "Listen pal, I wish . . ." John McCain with Mark Salter, *Worth the Fighting For: A Memoir* (New York: Random House, 2002) 62.

CHAPTER SIX: Success and Scandal

p. 57, "Well, only if he . . ." McCain with Salter, *Worth the Fighting For*, 123.

CHAPTER SEVEN: New World

p. 70, "Who are the ones . . ." Paul Alexander, *Man of*

the People: The Life of John McCain (New York: John Wiley & Sons, 2003), 144.

p. 73, "while some information remains . . ." Senate Select Committee on POW/MIA Affairs, "Report of the Senate Select Committee on POW?MIA Affairs," 103d Cong., 1st sess., 1993, S. Rep. 103-1, http://www.fas.org/irp/congress/1993_rpt/pow-exec.html.

CHAPTER EIGHT: Maverick

p. 78, "a constant and often . . ." McCain with Salter, *Worth the Fighting For*, 277.

p. 80, "More that 3000 children . . ." Alexander, *Man of the People*, 185.

CHAPTER NINE: Straight Talk

p. 85, "It is because I . . ." Alexander, *Man of the People*, 198.

p. 91, "a few self-appointed . . . is our message," Ibid., 290.

CHAPTER TEN: Another Try

p. 93, "I support him . . . themselves to America," Alexander, *Man of the People*, 324.

p. 96, "want their government back," Ibid., 377.

p. 97, "This is as serious . . ." Ibid., 358.

p. 100, "America is at war . . ." John McCain, "McCain: Nation Must Speak With One Voice Once We Determine Course Against Iraq," news release, October 2, 2002, http://mccain.senate.gov/press_office/view_article.cfm?id=452.

p. 102, "I believe the consequences . . ." John Heilprin, "McCain Says More Troops Needed in Iraq," Associated Press, November 19, 2006.

Bibliography

Alexander, Paul. *Man of the People: The Life of John McCain*. New York: John Wiley & Sons, 2003.

Heilprin, John. "McCain Says More Troops Needed in Iraq." Associated Press, November 19, 2006.

McCain, John, and Mark Salter. *Faith of My Fathers: A Family Memoir*. New York: Random House, 1999.

———.*Worth the Fighting For: A Memoir*. New York: Random House, 2002.

U.S. Congress. Senate. *Report of the Select Committee on POW/MIA Affairs*. 103d Cong., 1st sess., 1993. S. Rep. 103-1. http://www.fas.org/irp/congress/1993_rpt/pow-exec.html.

Timberg, Robert. *John McCain: An American Odyssey*. New York: Simon & Schuster, 1999.

Web sites

http://www.Mccain.senate.gov
Official site for the Republican senator from Arizona.

http://www.johnmccain.com
John McCain's 2008 campaign site includes a short biography and photo gallery, among other features.

http://topics.nytimes.com/top/reference/timestopics/people/m/john_mccain/
This *New York Times* page on John McCain links to hundreds of pages of online news articles, feature stories, and editorials written by *Times* reporters about Senator McCain, dating back to 1985.

Index

Babbit, Bruce, 52, 71
Bush, George H. W., 57-60, *58*, 67, 69-71, 78, 83
Bush, George W., 82, 84-92, *90*, 93-98, *99*, 100-101, 103

Carter, Jimmy, 40
Castro, Fidel, 20
Cheney, Dick, 60
Clinton, Bill, 39, 71, 73, 76-82, *77*, 83-84
Cohen, William, 39, 46
Cronkite, Walter, 49-50, *49*

Dole, Bob, 57, 79, 83
Dukakis, Michael, 58

Eisenhower, Dwight, *16*, 17

Feingold, Russ, 81, *81*

Goldwater, Barry, 51
Gorbachev, Mikhail, 67-68
Gramm, Phil, 79

Hart, Gary, 39, 46
Hensley, Cindy (wife), 41-44, *42*, 46, 50, 63, *74*, 75, *86*, 89
Hussein, Saddam, 68-70, 78, 98-101

Johnson, Lyndon, 19, 25-26, 32

Keating, Charles, 62-65, *62*
Keating Five, 61-65, 66, 70, 83
Kennedy, John, 20-21
Kerry, John, 71-73, *72*, 77, 101
Khomeini, Ayatollah Ruholla, 52
Khrushchev, Nikita, 20-21

Laden, Osama bin, 98

McCain, James (son), *74*, 75
McCain, Bridget (daughter), *74*, 75
McCain, John Sidney "Slew" (grandfather), 9-11, *10*, 38
McCain, John Sidney II (father), 9-11, *10*, 16, *17*, 29, 31-32, 38, 41, 68
McCain, John Sidney III, *8*, *17*, *21*, *27*, *29*, *30*, *34*, *36*, *37*, *42*, *51*, *64*, *72*, *74*, *77*, *80*, *81*, *84*, *86*, *88*, *90*, *94*, *99*, *100*, *102*
  Birth, 10
  Captured in Vietnam, 26-28
  Death of father, 41
  Divorced from Carol Shepp, 39
  Elected to House of Representatives, 45
  Elected to Senate, 52
  Marriage to Carol Shepp, 22
  Marriage to Cindy Hensley, 41
McCain, John Sidney IV (son), *74*, 75

McCain, Meghan (daughter), 50, *74*, 75
McCain, Sydney (daughter), 22
McCain-Feingold bill, 81, 84, 95-98
Minh, Ho Chi, *18*, 19

Nixon, Richard, 33, 36, *37*,
Noriega, Manuel, 67, *67*

Poindexter, John, 54

Quayle, Dan, 57

Ravenel, William, 13
Reagan, Ronald, 40-41, 46-49, 52-54, 68
Rhodes, John, 43
Robertson, Pat, 91
Rumsfeld, Donald, 101

Shepp, Carol (wife), 22, 25, 35-36, *36*, 38-39

U.S.S. *Forrestal, 22, 23*, 25
U.S.S. *Oriskany* 25
Tower, John, 59-61, *59*, 66
Truman, Harry, 9

Wright, Roberta (mother), 10, 16, *17*